CLIFFSCOMPLETE™

Shakespeare's

A Midsummer Night's Dream

Edited and commentary by Michael McMahon

Teacher of English literature

Complete Text + Commentary + Glossary

Wiley Publishing, Inc.

Shakespeare's

A Midsummer Night's Dream

About the Author

Michael McMahon taught literature in public and private schools in England and now writes full time.

Publisher's Acknowledgments

Editorial

Project Editor: S. L. Fugit

Acquisitions Editor: Gregory W. Tubach

Copy Editor: Robert Annis

Editorial Manager: Jennifer Ehrlich

Special Help: Melissa Bennett, Jennifer Young

Composition

Proofreader: Laura L. Bowman

Indexer: Sharon Hilgenberg

Wiley Indianapolis Composition Services

CliffsComplete™ Shakespeare's *A Midsummer Night's Dream*
Published by
Wiley Publishing, Inc.
111 River Street
Hoboken, NJ 07030
www.wiley.com

Copyright © 2001 Wiley Publishing, Inc. New York, New York

Library of Congress Control Number: 2001088154

ISBN: 978-0-7645-8725-2

Printed in the United States of America

10 9 8

1O/RV/QS/QY/IN

CLIFFSCOMPLETE™

**Shakespeare's
A Midsummer Night's Dream**

CONTENTS AT A GLANCE

CLIFFSCOMPLETE™

Shakespeare's
A Midsummer Night's Dream

TABLE OF CONTENTS

Shakespeare's
A MIDSUMMER NIGHT'S DREAM

INTRODUCTION TO WILLIAM SHAKESPEARE

William Shakespeare, or the "Bard" as people fondly call him, permeates almost all aspects of our society. He can be found in our classrooms, on our televisions, in our theatres, and in our cinemas. Speaking to us through his plays, Shakespeare comments on his life and culture, as well as our own. Actors still regularly perform his plays on the modern stage and screen. The 1990s, for example, saw the release of cinematic versions of *Romeo and Juliet, Hamlet, Othello, A Midsummer Night's Dream,* and many more of his works.

In addition to the popularity of Shakespeare's plays as he wrote them, other writers have modernized his works to attract new audiences. For example, *West Side Story* places *Romeo and Juliet* in New York City, and *A Thousand Acres* sets *King Lear* in Iowa corn country. Beyond adaptations and productions, his life and works have captured our cultural imagination. The twentieth century witnessed the production of a play about two minor characters from Shakespeare's *Hamlet* in *Rosencrantz and Guildenstern are Dead* and a fictional movie about Shakespeare's early life and poetic inspiration in *Shakespeare in Love.*

Despite his monumental presence in our culture, Shakespeare remains enigmatic. He does not tell us which plays he wrote alone, on which plays he collaborated with other playwrights, or which versions of his plays to read and perform. Furthermore, with only a handful of documents available about his life, he does not tell us much about Shakespeare the person, forcing critics and scholars to look to historical references to uncover the true-life great dramatist.

Anti-Stratfordians—modern scholars who question the authorship of Shakespeare's plays—have used this lack of information to argue that William Shakespeare either never existed, or if he did exist, did not write any of the plays attributed to him. They believe that another historical figure, such as Francis Bacon or Queen Elizabeth I, used the name

An engraved portrait of Shakespeare by an unknown artist, ca. 1607.
Culver Pictures, Inc./SuperStock

as a cover. Whether or not a man named William Shakespeare ever actually existed is ultimately secondary to the recognition that the group of plays bound together by that name does exist and continues to educate, enlighten, and entertain us.

Family life

Though scholars are unsure of the exact date of Shakespeare's birth, records indicate that his parents, Mary and John Shakespeare, baptized him on April 26, 1564, in the small provincial town of Stratford-upon-Avon, so named because it sat on the banks of the Avon river. Because common practice was to baptize infants a few days after they were born, scholars generally recognize April 23, 1564, as Shakespeare's birthday. Coincidentally, April 23 is the day of St. George, the patron saint of England, as well as the day upon which Shakespeare would die 52 years later. William was the third of Mary and John's eight children and the first of four sons. The house where scholars believe Shakespeare was born stands on Henley Street, and, despite many modifications over the years, you can still visit it today.

Shakespeare's father

Prior to Shakespeare's birth, John Shakespeare lived in Snitterfield, where he married Mary Arden, the daughter of his landlord. After moving to Stratford in 1552, he worked as a glover, a moneylender, and a dealer in agricultural products such as wool and grain. He also pursued public office and achieved a variety of posts including bailiff, Stratford's highest elected position, equivalent to a small town's mayor. At the height of his career, sometime near 1576, he petitioned the Herald's Office for a coat of arms and thus the right to be a gentleman. But the rise from the middle class to the gentry did not come right away, and the costly petition expired without being granted.

About this time, John Shakespeare mysteriously fell into financial difficulty. He became involved in

Shakespeare's birthplace.
SuperStock

serious litigation, was assessed heavy fines, and even lost his seat on the town council. Some scholars suggest that this decline could have resulted from religious discrimination because the Shakespeare family may have supported Catholicism, the practice of which was illegal in England. However, other scholars point out that not all religious dissenters (both Catholics and radical Puritans) lost their posts due to their religion. Whatever the cause of his decline, John did regain some prosperity toward the end of his life. In 1596, the Herald's Office granted the Shakespeare family a coat of arms at the petition of William, by now a successful playwright in London. And John, prior to his death in 1601, regained his seat on Stratford's town council.

Childhood and education

Our understanding of William Shakespeare's childhood in Stratford is primarily speculative because children do not often appear in the legal records from which many scholars attempt to reconstruct Shakespeare's life. Based on his father's local prominence, scholars speculate that Shakespeare most likely attended King's New School, a school that usually employed Oxford graduates and was generally well respected. Shakespeare would have started petty school—the rough equivalent to modern preschool—at the age of four or five. He would have learned to read on a hornbook, which was a sheet of parchment or paper on which the alphabet and the

Lord's Prayer were written. This sheet was framed in wood and covered with a transparent piece of horn for durability. After two years in petty school, he would have transferred to grammar school, where his school day would have probably lasted from 6 or 7 o'clock in the morning (depending on the time of year) until 5 o'clock in the evening, with only a handful of holidays.

While in grammar school, Shakespeare would primarily have studied Latin, reciting and reading the works of classical Roman authors such as Plautus, Ovid, Seneca, and Horace. Traces of these authors' works can be seen in his dramatic texts. Toward his last years in grammar school, Shakespeare would have acquired some basic skills in Greek as well. Thus the remark made by Ben Jonson, Shakespeare's well-educated friend and contemporary playwright, that Shakespeare knew "small Latin and less Greek" is accurate. Jonson is not saying that when Shakespeare left grammar school he was only semiliterate; he merely indicates that Shakespeare did not attend any university, where he would have gained more Latin and Greek instruction.

Wife and children

When Shakespeare became an adult, the historical records documenting his existence began to increase. In November 1582, at the age of 18, he married 26-year-old Anne Hathaway from the nearby village of Shottery. The disparity in their ages, coupled with the fact that they baptized their first daughter, Susanna, only six months later in May 1583, has caused a great deal of modern speculation about the nature of their relationship. However, sixteenth-century conceptions of marriage differed slightly from modern notions. Though all marriages needed to be performed before a member of the clergy, many of Shakespeare's contemporaries believed that a couple could establish a relationship through a premarital contract by exchanging vows in front of witnesses. This contract removed the social stigma of pregnancy before marriage. (Shakespeare's plays

contain instances of marriage prompted by pregnancy, and *Measure for Measure* includes this kind of premarital contract.) Two years later, in February 1585, Shakespeare baptized his twins Hamnet and Judith. Hamnet would die at the age of 11 when Shakespeare was primarily living away from his family in London.

For seven years after the twins' baptism, the records remain silent on Shakespeare. At some point, he traveled to London and became involved with the theatre, but he could have been anywhere between 21 and 28 years old when he did. Though some have suggested that he may have served as an assistant to a schoolmaster at a provincial school, it seems likely that he went to London to become an actor, gradually becoming a playwright and gaining attention.

The plays: On stage and in print

The next mention of Shakespeare comes in 1592 by a university wit named Robert Greene when Shakespeare apparently was already a rising actor and playwright for the London stage. Greene, no longer a successful playwright, tried to warn other university wits about Shakespeare. He wrote:

> For there is an upstart crow, beautified with our feathers, that with his "Tiger's heart wrapped in a player's hide" supposes he is as well able to bombast out a blank verse as the best of you, and, being an absolute Johannes Factotum, is in his own conceit the only Shake-scene in a country.

This statement comes at a point in time when men without a university education, such as Shakespeare, were starting to compete as dramatists with the university wits. As many critics have pointed out, Greene's statement recalls a line from *3 Henry VI,* which reads, "O tiger's heart wrapped in a woman's hide!" (I.4.137). Greene's remark does not indicate that Shakespeare was generally disliked. On the contrary, another university wit, Thomas Nashe, wrote of the great theatrical success of *Henry VI,* and Henry Chettle, Greene's publisher, later printed a flattering apology to Shakespeare. What Greene's statement does show us is that Shakespeare's reputation for poetry had reached enough of a prominence to provoke the envy of a failing competitor.

In the following year, 1593, the government closed London's theatres due to an outbreak of the bubonic plague. Publication history suggests that during this closure, Shakespeare may have written his two narrative poems, *Venus and Adonis,* published in 1593, and *The Rape of Lucrece,* published in 1594. These are the only two works that Shakespeare seems to have helped into print; each carries a dedication by Shakespeare to Henry Wriothesley, Earl of Southampton.

Stage success

When the theatres reopened in 1594, Shakespeare joined the Lord Chamberlain's Men, an acting company. Though uncertain about the history of his early dramatic works, scholars believe that by this point he had written *The Two Gentlemen of Verona, The Taming of the Shrew, the Henry VI trilogy,* and *Titus Andronicus.* During his early years in the theatre, he primarily wrote history plays, with his romantic comedies emerging in the 1590s. Even at this early stage in his career, Shakespeare was a success. In 1597, he was able to purchase New Place, one of the two largest houses in Stratford, and secure a coat of arms for his family.

In 1597, the lease expired on the Lord Chamberlain's playhouse, called The Theatre. Because the owner of The Theatre refused to renew the lease, the acting company was forced to perform at various playhouses until the 1599 opening of the now famous Globe Theatre, which was literally built with lumber from The Theatre. (The Globe, later destroyed by fire, has recently been reconstructed in London and can be visited today.)

Recent scholars suggest that Shakespeare's great tragedy, *Julius Caesar,* may have been the first of Shakespeare's plays performed in the original playhouse. When this open-air theatre on the Thames River opened, financial papers list Shakespeare's name as one of the principal investors. Already an actor and a playwright, Shakespeare was now becoming a "Company Man." This new status allowed him to share in the profits of the theatre rather than merely getting paid for his plays, some of which publishers were beginning to release in quarto format.

Publications

A quarto was a small, inexpensive book typically used for leisure books such as

A ground plan of London after the fire of 1666, drawn by Marcus Willemsz Doornik. Guildhall Library, London/AKG, Berlin/SuperStock

plays; the term itself indicates that the printer folded the paper four times. The modern day equivalent of a quarto would be a paperback. In contrast, the first collected works of Shakespeare were in folio format, which means that the printer folded each sheet only once. Scholars call the collected edition of Shakespeare's works the First Folio. A folio was a larger and more prestigious book than a quarto, and printers generally reserved the format for works such as the Bible.

No evidence exists that Shakespeare participated in the publication of any of his plays. Members of Shakespeare's acting company printed the First Folio seven years after Shakespeare's death. Generally, playwrights wrote their works to be performed on stage, and publishing them was a novel innovation at the time. Shakespeare probably would not have thought of them as books in the way we do. In fact, as a principal investor in the acting company (which purchased the play as well as the exclusive right to perform it), he may not have even thought of them as his own. He would probably have thought of his plays as belonging to the company.

For this reason, scholars have generally characterized most quartos printed before the Folio as "bad" by arguing that printers pirated the plays and published them illegally. How would a printer have received a pirated copy of a play? The theories range from someone stealing a copy to an actor (or actors) selling the play by relating it from memory to a printer. Many times, major differences exist between a quarto version of the play and a folio version, causing uncertainty about which is Shakespeare's true creation. Hamlet, for example, is almost twice as long in the Folio as in quarto versions. Recently, scholars have come to realize the value of the different versions. The Norton Shakespeare, for example, includes all three versions of *King Lear*—the quarto, the folio, and the conflated version (the combination of the quarto and folio).

Prolific productions

The first decade of the 1600s witnessed the publication of additional quartos as well as the production of most of Shakespeare's great tragedies, with *Julius Caesar* appearing in 1599 and *Hamlet* in 1600–1601. After the death of Queen Elizabeth in 1603, the Lord Chamberlain's Men became the King's Men under James I, Elizabeth's successor. Around the time of this transition in the English monarchy, the famous tragedy *Othello* (1603–1604) was most likely written and performed, followed closely by *King Lear* (1605–1606), *Antony and Cleopatra* (1606), and *Macbeth* (1606) in the next two years.

Shakespeare's name also appears as a major investor in the 1609 acquisition of an indoor theatre known as the Blackfriars. This last period of Shakespeare's career, which includes plays that considered the acting conditions both at the Blackfriars and the open-air Globe Theatre, consists primarily of romances or tragicomedies such as *The Winter's Tale* and *The Tempest*. On June 29, 1613, during a performance of *All is True,* or *Henry VIII,* the thatching on top of the Globe caught fire and the playhouse burned to the ground. After this incident, the King's Men moved solely into the indoor Blackfriars Theatre.

Final days

During the last years of his career, Shakespeare collaborated on a couple of plays with contemporary dramatist John Fletcher, even possibly coming out of retirement, which scholars believe began sometime in 1613, to work on *The Two Noble Kinsmen* (1613–1614). Three years later, Shakespeare died on April 23, 1616. Though the exact cause of death remains unknown, a vicar from Stratford in the mid-seventeenth-century wrote in his diary that Shakespeare, perhaps celebrating the marriage of his daughter, Judith, contracted a fever during a night of revelry with fellow literary figures Ben Jonson and Michael Drayton. Regardless, Shakespeare may have felt his death was imminent in March of that year because he altered his will. Interestingly, his will mentions no book or theatrical manuscripts, perhaps indicating the lack of value that he put on printed versions of his dramatic works and their status as company property.

Seven years after Shakespeare's death, John Heminges and Henry Condell, fellow members of the King's Men, published his collected works. In their preface, they claim that they are publishing the true versions of Shakespeare's plays partially as a response to the previous quarto printings of 18 of his plays, most of these with multiple printings. This Folio contains 36 plays to which scholars generally add *Pericles* and *The Two Noble Kinsmen*. This volume of Shakespeare's plays began the process of constructing Shakespeare not only as England's national poet but also as a monumental figure whose plays would continue to captivate imaginations at the end of the millennium with no signs of stopping. Ben Jonson's prophetic line about Shakespeare in the First Folio—"He was not of an age, but for all time!"—certainly holds true.

Chronology of Shakespeare's plays

1590–1591	*The Two Gentlemen of Verona*
	The Taming of the Shrew
1591	*2 Henry VI*
	3 Henry VI
1592	*1 Henry VI*
	Titus Andronicus
1592–1593	*Richard III*
	Venus and Adonis
1593–1594	*The Rape of Lucrece*
1594	*The Comedy of Errors*
1594–1595	*Love's Labour's Lost*
1595	*Richard II*
	Romeo and Juliet
	A Midsummer Night's Dream
1595–1596	*Love's Labour's Won*
	(This manuscript was lost.)

1596	*King John*
1596–1597	*The Merchant of Venice*
	1 Henry IV
1597–1598	*The Merry Wives of Windsor*
	2 Henry IV
1598	*Much Ado About Nothing*
1598–1599	*Henry V*
1599	*Julius Caesar*
1599–1600	*As You Like It*
1600–1601	*Hamlet*
1601	*Twelfth Night, or What You Will*
1602	*Troilus and Cressida*
1593–1603	*Sonnets*
1603	*Measure for Measure*
1603–1604	*A Lover's Complaint*
	Othello
1604–1605	*All's Well That Ends Well*
1605	*Timon of Athens*
1605–1606	*King Lear*
1606	*Macbeth*
	Antony and Cleopatra
1607	*Pericles*
1608	*Coriolanus*
1609	*The Winter's Tale*
1610	*Cymbeline*
1611	*The Tempest*
1612–1613	*Cardenio* (with John Fletcher; this manuscript was lost.)
1613	*All is True* (Henry VIII)
1613–1614	*The Two Noble Kinsmen* (with John Fletcher)

This chronology is derived from Stanley Wells's and Gary Taylor's *William Shakespeare: A Textual Companion*, which is listed in the "Works consulted" section that follows.

A note on Shakespeare's language

Readers encountering Shakespeare for the first time usually find Early Modern English difficult to understand. Yet, rather than serving as a barrier to Shakespeare, the richness of this language should form part of one's appreciation of the Bard.

One of the first things readers usually notice about the language is the use of pronouns. Like the King James Version of the Bible, Shakespeare's pronouns are slightly different from our own and can cause confusion. Words like "thou" (you), "thee" and "ye" (objective cases of you), and "thy" and "thine" (your/yours) appear throughout Shakespeare's plays. You may need a little time to get used to these changes. You can find the definitions for other words that commonly cause confusion in the notes column on the right side of each page in this edition.

Iambic pentameter

Though Shakespeare sometimes wrote in prose, he wrote most of his plays in poetry, specifically blank verse. Blank verse consists of lines in unrhymed iambic pentameter. Iambic refers to the stress patterns of the line. An iamb is an element of sound that consists of two beats—the first unstressed (da) and the second stressed (DA). A good example of an iambic line is Hamlet's famous line "To be or not to be," in which you do not stress "to," "or," and "to," but you do stress "be," "not," and "be." Pentameter refers to the meter or number of stressed syllables in a line. Penta-meter has five stressed syllables. Thus, Juliet's line "But soft, what light through yonder window breaks?" (II.2.2) is a good example of an iambic pentameter line.

Wordplay

Shakespeare's language is also verbally rich as he, along with many dramatists of his period, had a fondness for wordplay. This wordplay often takes the form of double meanings, called puns, where a word can mean more than one thing in a given context. Shakespeare often employs these puns as a way of illustrating the distance between what is on the surface—apparent meanings—and what meanings lie underneath. Though recognizing these puns may be difficult at first, the notes in the far right column point many of them out to you.

If you are encountering Shakespeare's plays for the first time, the following reading tips may help ease you into the plays. Shakespeare's lines were meant to be spoken; therefore, reading them aloud or speaking them should help with comprehension. Also, though most of the lines are poetic, do not forget to read complete sentences—move from period to period as well as from line to line. Although Shakespeare's language can be difficult at first, the rewards of immersing yourself in the richness and fluidity of the lines are immeasurable.

Works consulted

For more information on Shakespeare's life and works, see the following:

Bevington, David, ed. *The Complete Works of Shakespeare.* New York: Longman, 1997.

Evans, G.Blakemore, ed. *The Riverside Shakespeare.* Boston: Houghton Mifflin Co., 1997.

Greenblatt, Stephen, ed. *The Norton Shakespeare.* New York: W.W. Norton and Co., 1997.

Kastan, David Scott, ed. *A Companion to Shakespeare.* Oxford: Blackwell, 1999.

McDonald, Russ. *The Bedford Companion to Shakespeare: An Introduction with Documents.* Boston: Bedford-St. Martin's Press, 1996.

Wells, Stanley and Gary Taylor. *William Shakespeare: A Textual Companion.* New York: W.W. Norton and Co., 1997.

INTRODUCTION TO EARLY MODERN ENGLAND

William Shakespeare (1564–1616) lived during a period in England's history that people have generally referred to as the English Renaissance. The term *renaissance*, meaning rebirth, was applied to this period of English history as a way of celebrating what was perceived as the rapid development of art, literature, science, and politics: in many ways, the rebirth of classical Rome.

Recently, scholars have challenged the name "English Renaissance" on two grounds. First, some scholars argue that the term should not be used because women did not share in the advancements of English culture during this time period; their legal status was still below that of men. Second, other scholars have challenged the basic notion that this period saw a sudden explosion of culture. A rebirth of civilization suggests that the previous period of time was not civilized. This second group of scholars sees a much more gradual transition between the Middle Ages and Shakespeare's time.

Some people use the terms *Elizabethan* and *Jacobean* when referring to periods of the sixteenth and seventeenth centuries. These terms correspond to the reigns of Elizabeth I (1558–1603) and James I (1603–1625). The problem with these terms is that they do not cover large spans of time; for example, Shakespeare's life and career spans both monarchies.

Scholars are now beginning to replace Renaissance with the term *Early Modern* when referring to this time period, but people still use both terms interchangeably. The term Early Modern recognizes that this period established many of the foundations of our modern culture. Though critics still disagree about the exact dates of the period, generally, the dates range from 1450 to 1750. Thus, Shakespeare's life clearly falls within the Early Modern period.

Shakespeare's plays live on in our culture, but we must remember that Shakespeare's culture differed greatly from our own. Though his understanding of human nature and relationships seems to apply to our modern lives, we must try to understand the world he lived in so we can better understand his plays. This introduction helps you do just that. It examines the intellectual, religious, political, and social contexts of Shakespeare's work before turning to the importance of the theatre and the printing press.

Intellectual context

Generally, people in Early Modern England looked at the universe, the human body, and science very differently from the way we do today. But while we do not share their same beliefs, we must not think of people during Shakespeare's time as lacking in intelligence or education. Discoveries made during the Early Modern period concerning the universe and the human body provide the basis of modern science.

Cosmology

One subject we view very differently than Early Modern thinkers is cosmology. Shakespeare's contemporaries believed in the astronomy of Ptolemy, an intellectual from Alexandria in the second century A.D. Ptolemy thought that the earth stood at the center of the universe, surrounded by nine concentric rings. The celestial bodies circled the earth in the following order: the moon, Mercury, Venus, the sun, Mars, Jupiter, Saturn, and the stars. The entire system was controlled by the *primum mobile*, or Prime Mover, which initiated and maintained the movement of the celestial bodies. No one had yet discovered the last three planets in our the solar system: Uranus, Neptune, and Pluto.

In 1543, Nicolaus Copernicus published his theory of a sun-based solar system, in which the sun stood at the center and the planets revolved around it. Though this theory appeared prior to Shakespeare's birth, people didn't really start to change their minds until 1610, when Galileo used his telescope to confirm Copernicus's theory. David Bevington asserts in the general introduction to his edition of Shakespeare's works that during most of Shakespeare's writing career, the cosmology of the universe was in question, and this sense of uncertainty influences some of his plays.

Universal hierarchy

Closely related to Ptolemy's hierarchical view of the universe is a hierarchical conception of the Earth (sometimes referred to as the Chain of Being). During the Early Modern period, many people believed that all of creation was organized hierarchically. God existed at the top, followed by the angels, men, women, animals, plants, and rocks. (Because all women were thought to exist below all men on the chain, you can easily imagine the confusion that Elizabeth I caused when she became queen of England. She was literally "out of order," an expression that still exists in our society.) Though the concept of this hierarchy is a useful one when beginning to study Shakespeare, keep in mind that distinctions in this hierarchical view were not always clear and that one should not reduce all Early Modern thinking to a simple chain.

Elements and humors

The belief in a hierarchical scheme of existence created a comforting sense of order and balance that carried over into science as well. Shakespeare's contemporaries generally accepted that four different elements composed everything in the universe: earth, air, water, and fire. People associated these four elements with four qualities of being. These qualities—hot, cold, moist, and dry—appeared in different combinations in the elements. For example, air was hot and moist; water was cold and moist; earth was cold and dry; and fire was hot and dry.

In addition, people believed that the human body contained all four elements in the form of *humors*—blood, phlegm, yellow bile, and black bile—each of which corresponded to an element. Blood corresponded to air (hot and moist), phlegm to water (cold and moist), yellow bile to fire (hot and dry), and black bile to earth (cold and dry). When someone was sick, physicians generally believed that the patient's humors were not in the proper balance. For example, if someone were diagnosed with an abundance of blood, the physician would bleed the patient (using leeches or cutting the skin) in order to restore the balance.

Shakespeare's contemporaries also believed that the humors determined personality and temperament. If a person's dominant humor was blood, he was considered light-hearted. If dominated by yellow bile (or choler), that person was irritable. The dominance of phlegm led a person to be dull and kind. And if black bile prevailed, he was melancholy or sad. Thus, people of Early Modern England often used the humors to explain behavior and emotional outbursts. Throughout Shakespeare's plays, he uses the concept of the humors to define and explain various characters.

The Reformation

Prior to the early sixteenth century in Europe, until the Protestant Reformation, the only Christian church was the Catholic, or "universal," church. Beginning in Europe in the early sixteenth century, religious thinkers such as Martin Luther and John Calvin, who claimed that the Roman Catholic Church had become corrupt and was no longer following the word of God, began what has become known as the *Protestant Reformation*. The Protestants ("protestors") believed in salvation by faith rather than works. They also believed in the primacy of the Bible and advocated giving all people access to reading the Bible.

Many of the English people initially resisted Protestant ideas. However, the Reformation in England began in 1527 during the reign of Henry VIII, prior to Shakespeare's birth. In that year, Henry VIII decided to divorce his wife, Catherine of Aragon, for her failure to produce a male heir. (Only one of their children, Mary, survived past infancy.) Rome denied Henry's petitions for a divorce, forcing him to divorce Catherine without the Church's approval, which he did in 1533.

A portrait of King Henry VIII, artist unknown, ca. 1542.
National Portrait Gallery, London/SuperStock

The Act of Supremacy

The following year, the Pope excommunicated Henry VIII while Parliament confirmed his divorce and the legitimacy of his new marriage through the *Act of Succession*. Later in 1534, Parliament passed the *Act of Supremacy*, naming Henry the "Supreme Head of the Church in England." Henry continued to persecute both radical Protestant reformers and Catholics who remained loyal to Rome.

Henry VIII's death in 1547 brought Edward VI, his 10-year-old son by Jane Seymour (the king's third wife), to the throne. This succession gave Protestant reformers the chance to solidify their break with the Catholic Church. During Edward's reign, Archbishop Thomas Cranmer established the foundation for the Anglican Church (Church of England) through his 42 articles of religion. He also wrote the

first *Book of Common Prayer*, adopted in 1549, which was the official text for worship services in England.

Bloody Mary

Catholics continued to be persecuted until 1553, when the sickly Edward VI died and was succeeded by Mary, his half-sister and the Catholic daughter of Catherine of Aragon. The reign of Mary witnessed the reversal of religion in England through the restoration of Catholic authority and obedience to Rome. Protestants were executed in large numbers, which earned the monarch the nickname *Bloody Mary*. Many Protestants fled to Europe to escape persecution.

Elizabeth I, the daughter of Henry VIII and Anne Boleyn, outwardly complied with the mandated Catholicism during her half-sister Mary's reign, but she restored Protestantism when she took the throne in 1558 after Mary's death. Thus, in the space of a single decade, England's throne passed from Protestant to Catholic to Protestant, with each change carrying serious and deadly consequences.

Though Elizabeth reigned in relative peace from 1558 to her death in 1603, religion was still a serious concern for her subjects. During Shakespeare's life, a great deal of religious dissent existed in England. Many Catholics, who remained loyal to Rome and their church, were persecuted for their beliefs. At the other end of the spectrum, the Puritans were persecuted for their belief that the Reformation was not complete. (The English pejoratively applied the term *Puritan* to religious groups that wanted to continue purifying the English church by such measures as removing the *episcopacy*, or the structure of bishops.)

The Great Bible

One thing agreed upon by both the Anglicans and Puritans was the importance of a Bible written in English. Translated by William Tyndale in 1525, the first authorized Bible in English, published in 1539, was known as the Great Bible. An English version of the Bible made it easier for everyone to read and interpret the scriptures in their own way. This became an especially dangerous thing as women began to realize that a man's supremacy was not an act of God but an act of men. So, in 1543, an "Act for the Advancement of True Religion" was established. This Act forbade women to read the Bible in English. This Bible was later revised during Elizabeth's reign into what was known as the Bishop's Bible. As Stephen Greenblatt points out in his introduction to the *Norton Shakespeare*, Shakespeare would probably have been familiar with both the Bishop's Bible, heard aloud in Mass, and the Geneva Bible, which was written by English exiles in Geneva. The last authorized Bible produced during Shakespeare's lifetime came within the last decade of his life when James I's commissioned edition, known as the King James Bible, appeared in 1611.

Political context

Politics and religion were closely related in Shakespeare's England. Both of the monarchs under whom Shakespeare lived had to deal with religious and political dissenters.

Elizabeth I

Despite being a Protestant, Elizabeth I tried to take a middle road on the religious question of religion. She allowed Catholics to practice their religion in private as long as they outwardly appeared Anglican and remained loyal to the throne.

Elizabeth's monarchy was one of absolute supremacy. Believing in the divine right of kings, she styled herself as being appointed by God to rule England. To oppose the Queen's will was the equivalent of opposing God's will. Known as *passive obedience*, this doctrine did not allow any opposition even to a tyrannical monarch because God had appointed the

A portrait of Elizabeth I by George Gower, ca. 1588. National Portrait Gallery, London/SuperStock

king or queen for reasons unknown to His subjects on earth. However, as Bevington notes, Elizabeth's power was not as absolute as her rhetoric suggested. Parliament, already well established in England, reserved some power, such as the authority to levy taxes, for itself.

Elizabeth I lived in a society that restricted women from possessing any political or personal autonomy and power. As queen, Elizabeth violated and called into question many of the prejudices and practices against women. In a way, her society forced her to "overcome" her sex in order to rule effectively. Although her position did nothing to increase the status of women in England, her strength and boldness perhaps served as a prototype for some of Shakespeare's more powerful women, such as Kate in *The Taming of the Shrew*, or those who express independence of purpose, such as Hermia in *A Midsummer Night's Dream*.

One of the rhetorical strategies that Elizabeth adopted in order to rule effectively was to separate her position as monarch of England from her natural body—to separate her *body politic* from her *body natural.* In addition, throughout her reign, Elizabeth brilliantly negotiated between domestic and foreign factions—some of whom were anxious about a female monarch and wanted her to marry—appeasing both sides without ever committing to one.

She remained unmarried throughout her 45-year reign, partially by styling herself as the Virgin Queen whose purity represented England herself. Her refusal to marry and her habit of hinting and promising marriage with suitors both foreign and domestic helped Elizabeth maintain internal and external peace. Not marrying allowed her to retain her independence, but it left the succession of the English throne in question. In 1603, on her deathbed, she named James VI, King of Scotland and son of her cousin Mary, as her successor.

James I

When he assumed the English crown, James VI of Scotland became James I of England. (Some historians refer to him as James VI and I.) Like Elizabeth, James was a strong believer in the divine right of kings and their absolute authority.

Upon his arrival in London to claim the English throne, James made his plans to unite Scotland and England clear. However, a long-standing history of enmity existed between the two countries. Partially as a result of this history and the influx of Scottish courtiers into English society, anti-Scottish prejudice abounded in England. When James asked Parliament for the title of "King of Great Britain," he was denied.

As scholars such as Bevington have pointed out, James was less successful than Elizabeth was in negotiating between the different religious and political factions in England. Although he was a Protestant, he began to have problems with the Puritan sect of the House of Commons, which ultimately led to a rift between the court (which also started to have Catholic sympathies) and the Parliament. This rift between the monarchy and Parliament eventually escalated into the Civil War that would erupt during the reign of James's son, Charles I.

In spite of its difficulties with Parliament, James's court was a site of wealth, luxury, and extravagance. James I commissioned elaborate feasts, masques, and pageants, and in doing so he more than doubled the royal debt. Stephen Greenblatt suggests that Shakespeare's *The Tempest* may reflect this extravagance through Prospero's magnificent banquet and accompanying masque. Reigning from 1603 to 1625, James I remained the king of England throughout the last years of Shakespeare's life.

Social context

Shakespeare's England divided itself roughly into two social classes: the aristocrats (or nobility) and everyone else. The primary distinctions between these two classes were ancestry, wealth, and power. Simply put, the aristocrats were the only ones who possessed all three.

Aristocrats were born with their wealth, but the growth of trade and the development of skilled professions began to provide wealth for those not born with it. Although the notion of a middle class did not begin to develop until after Shakespeare's death, the possibility of some social mobility did exist in Early Modern England. Shakespeare himself used the wealth gained from the theatre to move into the lower ranks of the aristocracy by securing a coat of arms for his family.

Shakespeare was not unique in this movement, but not all people received the opportunity to increase their social status. Members of the aristocracy feared this social movement, and, as a result, promoted harsh laws of apprenticeship and fashion, restricting certain styles of dress and material. These laws dictated that only the aristocracy could wear certain articles of clothing, colors, and materials. Though enforcement was a difficult task, the Early Modern aristocracy considered dressing above one's station a moral and ethical violation.

The status of women

The legal status of women did not allow them much public or private autonomy. English society functioned on a system of patriarchy and hierarchy (see "Social Context" earlier in this introduction), which means that men controlled society beginning with the individual family. In fact, the family metaphorically corresponded to the state. For example, the husband was the king of his family. His authority to control his family was absolute and based on divine right, similar to that of the country's king. People also saw the family itself differently than today, considering apprentices and servants part of the whole family.

The practice of *primogeniture*—a system of inheritance that passed all of a family's wealth through the first male child—accompanied this system of patriarchy. Thus women did not generally inherit their family's wealth and titles. In the absence of a male heir, some women, such as Queen Elizabeth, did. But after women married, they lost almost all of their already limited legal rights, such as the right to inherit, to own property, and to sign contracts. In all likelihood, Elizabeth I would have lost much of her power and authority if she married.

Furthermore, women did not generally receive an education outside of the home and could not enter certain professions, including acting. Instead, society continued to relegate women to the domestic sphere of the home.

It will not come as a surprise, then, that male characters tend to dominate the females in *A Midsummer Night's Dream*. Theseus won Hippolyta by overcoming her and her army in battle: "I woo'd thee with my sword, / And won thy love

doing thee injuries." His advice to Hermia that "To you, your father should be as a god" and that Hermia should marry as her father directs would have raised few eyebrows in Early Modern England. Similarly, Oberon's decision to punish Titania for refusing to hand over the Indian child to be his page would have been seen as perfectly reasonable by Shakespeare's audience.

Daily life

Daily life in Early Modern England began before sun-up—exactly how early depended on one's station in life. A servant's responsibilities usually included preparing the house for the day. Families usually possessed limited living space, and even among wealthy families multiple family members tended to share a small number of rooms, suggesting that privacy may not have been important or practical.

Working through the morning, Elizabethans usually had lunch about noon. This midday meal was the primary meal of the day, much like dinner is for modern families. The workday usually ended around sundown or 5 p.m., depending on the season. Before an early bedtime, Elizabethans usually ate a light repast and then settled in for a couple of hours of reading (if the family members were literate and could bear the high cost of books) or socializing.

Mortality rates

Mortality rates in Early Modern England were high compared to our standards, especially among infants. Infection and disease ran rampant because physicians did not realize the need for antiseptics and sterile equipment. As a result, communicable diseases often spread very rapidly in cities, particularly London.

In addition, the bubonic plague frequently ravaged England, with two major outbreaks—from 1592–1594 and in 1603—occurring during Shakespeare's lifetime. People did not understand the plague and generally perceived it as God's punishment. (We now know that the plague was spread by fleas and could not be spread directly from human to human.) Without a cure or an understanding of what transmitted the disease, physicians could do nothing to stop the thousands of deaths that resulted from each outbreak. These outbreaks had a direct effect on Shakespeare's career, because the government often closed the theatres in an effort to impede the spread of the disease.

London life

In the sixteenth century, London, though small compared to modern cities, was the largest city in Europe, with a population of about 200,000 inhabitants in the city and surrounding suburbs. London was a crowded city without a sewer system, which facilitated epidemics such as the plague. In addition, crime rates were high in the city due to inefficient law enforcement and the lack of street lighting.

Despite these drawbacks, London was the cultural, political, and social heart of England. As the home of the monarch and most of England's trade, London was a bustling metropolis. Not surprisingly, a young Shakespeare moved to London to begin his professional career.

The theatre

Most theatres were not actually located within the city of London. Rather, theatre owners built them on the South bank of the Thames River (in Southwark) across from the city in order to avoid the strict regulations that applied within the city's walls. These restrictions stemmed from a mistrust of public performances as locations of plague and riotous behavior. Furthermore, because theatre performances took place during the day, they took laborers away from their jobs. Opposition to the theatres also came from Puritans who believed that they fostered immorality. Therefore, theatres moved out of the city, to areas near other sites of restricted activities, such as dog fighting, bear- and bull-baiting, and prostitution.

The recently reconstructed Globe Theatre.
Chris Parker/PAL

Despite the move, the theatre was not free from censorship or regulation. In fact, a branch of the government known as the Office of the Revels attempted to ensure that plays did not present politically or socially sensitive material. Prior to each performance, the Master of the Revels would read a complete text of each play, cutting out offending sections or, in some cases, not approving the play for public performance.

Performance spaces

Theatres in Early Modern England were quite different from our modern facilities. They were usually open-air, relying heavily on natural light and good weather. The rectangular stage extended out into an area that people called the *pit*—a circular, uncovered area about 70 feet in diameter. Audience members had two choices when purchasing admission to a theatre. Admission to the pit, where the lower classes (or *groundlings*) stood for the performances, was the cheaper option. People of wealth could purchase a seat in one of the three covered tiers of seats that ringed the pit. At full capacity, a public theatre in Early Modern England could hold between 2,000 and 3,000 people.

The stage, which projected into the pit and was raised about five feet above it, had a covered portion called the *heavens*. The heavens enclosed theatrical equipment for lowering and raising actors to and from the stage. A trapdoor in the middle of the stage provided theatrical graves for characters such as Ophelia, and also allowed ghosts, such as Banquo in *Macbeth*, to rise from the earth. A wall separated the back of the stage from the actors' dressing room, known as the *tiring house*. (In Act III, Scene 1 of *A Midsummer Night's Dream,* the Athenian workmen rehearse their play in the wood near Athens, and Quince chooses a "hawthorn brake" to serve as their "tiring house.") At each end of the wall stood a door for major entrances and exits. Above the wall and doors stood a gallery directly above the stage, reserved for the wealthiest spectators. Actors occasionally used this area when a performance called for a difference in height—for example, to represent Juliet's balcony or the walls of a besieged city. A good example of this type of theatre was the original Globe Theatre in London in which Shakespeare's company, The Lord Chamberlain's Men (later the King's Men), staged its plays. However, indoor theatres, such as the Blackfriars, differed slightly because the pit was filled with chairs that faced a rectangular stage. Because only the wealthy could afford the cost of admission, the public generally considered these theatres private.

Actors and staging

Performances in Shakespeare's England do not appear to have employed scenery. However, theatre companies developed their costumes with great care and expense. In fact, a playing company's costumes were its most valuable items. These extravagant costumes were the object of much controversy because some aristocrats feared that the actors could use them to disguise their social status on the streets of London.

Costumes also disguised a player's gender. All actors on the stage during Shakespeare's lifetime were men. Young boys whose voices had not reached maturity played female parts. This practice no doubt influenced Shakespeare's and his contemporary playwrights' thematic explorations of cross-dressing.

Shakespeare was a man of the theatre, and his relationship to the theatre pervades many of his plays including *A Midsummer Night's Dream,* in which there is a play-within-the-play that is much more than a mere subplot. Its inclusion allows Shakespeare to develop his interest in the difference between appearance and reality, a subject that lies at the heart of all drama.

Though historians have managed to reconstruct the appearance of the early modern theatre, such as the recent construction of the Globe in London, much of the information regarding how plays were performed during this era has been lost. Scholars of Early Modern

Shakespeare in Love *shows how the interior of the Globe would have appeared.*
The Everett Collection

theatre have turned to the scant external and internal stage directions in manuscripts in an effort to find these answers. While a hindrance for modern critics and scholars, the lack of detail about Early Modern performances has allowed modern directors and actors a great deal of flexibility and room to be creative.

The printing press

If not for the printing press, many Early Modern plays may not have survived until today. In Shakespeare's time, printers produced all books by *sheet*—a single large piece of paper that the printer would fold in order to produce the desired book size. For example, a folio required folding the sheet once, a quarto four times, an octavo eight, and so on. Sheets would be printed one side at a time; thus, printers had to simultaneously print multiple nonconsecutive pages.

In order to estimate what section of the text would be on each page, the printer would *cast off* copy. After the printer made these estimates, *compositors* would set the type upside down, letter by letter. This process of setting type produced textual errors, some of which a proofreader would catch. When a proofreader found an error, the compositors would fix the piece or pieces of type. Printers called corrections made after printing began *stop-press* corrections because they literally had to stop the press to fix the error. Because of the high cost of paper, printers would still sell the sheets printed before they made the correction.

Printers placed frames of text in the bed of the printing press and used them to imprint the paper. They then folded and grouped the sheets of paper into gatherings, after which the pages were ready for sale. The buyer had the option of getting the new play bound.

The printing process was crucial to the preservation of Shakespeare's works, but the printing of drama in Early Modern England was not a standardized practice. Many of the first editions of Shakespeare's plays appear in quarto format, and, until recently, scholars regarded them as "corrupt." In fact, scholars still debate how close a relationship exists between what appeared on the stage in the sixteenth and seventeenth centuries and what appears on the printed page. The inconsistent and scant appearance of stage directions, for example, makes it difficult to determine how close this relationship was.

It is known that the practice of the theatre allowed the alteration of plays by a variety of hands other than the author's, further complicating any efforts to extract what a playwright wrote and what was changed by either the players, the printers, or the government censors.

Shakespeare wrote his plays for the stage, and the existing published texts reflect the collaborative nature of the theatre as well as the unavoidable changes made during the printing process. A play's first written version would have been the author's *foul papers*, which invariably consisted of blotted lines and revised text. From there, a scribe would recopy the play and produce a *fair copy*. The theatre manager would then copy out and annotate this copy into a playbook (what people today call a *promptbook*).

At this point, scrolls of individual parts were copied out for actors to memorize. (Due to the high cost of paper, theatre companies could not afford to provide their actors with a complete copy of the play.) The government required the company to send the playbook to the Master of the Revels, the government official who would make any necessary changes or mark any passages considered unacceptable for performance.

Printers could have used any one of these copies to print a play. It cannot be determined whether a printer used the author's version, the modified theatrical version, the censored version, or a combination when printing a given play. Refer back to the "Publications" section of the Introduction to William

Shakespeare for further discussion of the impact that printing practices had on the understanding of Shakespeare's works.

Works cited

For more information regarding Early Modern England, consult the following works:

Bevington, David. "General Introduction." *The Complete Works of William Shakespeare.* Updated Fourth edition. New York: Longman, 1997.

Greenblatt, Stephen. "Shakespeare's World." *Norton Shakespeare.* New York: W.W. Norton and Co., 1997.

Kastan, David Scott, ed. *A Companion to Shakespeare.* Oxford: Blackwell, 1999.

McDonald, Russ. *The Bedford Companion to Shakespeare: An Introduction with Documents.* Boston: Bedford-St. Martin's Press, 1996.

INTRODUCTION TO *A MIDSUMMER NIGHT'S DREAM*

A Midsummer Night's Dream has long been one of Shakespeare's most popular plays. Its magical atmosphere, farcical plot, hilarious play-within-a-play, and general air of celebration have been enjoyed by nearly every generation since it was written.

As one of Shakespeare's early works, the play was probably first performed in 1595 or 1596. Some scholars believe that it was written for a specific occasion: a grand wedding, possibly the marriage of Elizabeth Carey and Thomas Berkeley on February 19, 1596, or of Elizabeth Vere and the Earl of Derby on January 26, 1595. Whether or not Shakespeare wrote *A Midsummer Night's Dream* for a particular wedding, the play certainly celebrates the idea of marriage. Its conflicts are resolved through marriage, and the entire last act is devoted to the festivities

following the triple wedding of Theseus and Hippolyta, Lysander and Hermia, and Demetrius and Helena.

The First Quarto edition of the play was published in 1600; the Second, in 1619. *A Midsummer Night's Dream* appeared in the First Folio of 1623, which was a collected edition of Shakespeare's plays assembled by two of the surviving members of his acting company. There are relatively few differences between these texts, and this CliffsComplete edition corresponds closely to the version accepted by most scholars today. The only differences between this and any other recent edition of the play are small details of punctuation, and the editor's decision to opt for the reading "Mote" rather than "Moth" for the name of one of the fairies, for reasons that are explained in the commentaries.

Shakespeare's sources

Shakespeare drew upon many elements from earlier literature and folklore in writing *A Midsummer Night's Dream,* but the result is much more than the sum of those parts. As always, he weaves his sources together to create a thoroughly new and independent work of art. Shakespeare does not simply re-tell other people's stories; he picks and chooses details from them that serve his own creative purpose. It is interesting to identify names, characters, and incidents that Shakespeare has lifted from earlier works, but it is much more useful to see how he has changed and adapted them to his own ends.

The story of Theseus and Hippolyta is found in Chaucer's *The Knight's Tale* and in Plutarch's *Life of Theseus,* translated by Sir Thomas North. Shakespeare uses elements of both, including the names of some of Chaucer's characters, Egeus and Philostrate. The idea of a quarrelling King and Queen of the Fairies probably also comes from Chaucer—from *The Merchant's Tale*—but Shakespeare's creative imagination links the two stories by inventing relationships between Oberon and Hippolyta and Titania and Theseus. Chaucer's version of the Pyramus and Thisbe story was also known to Shakespeare: The tale that Shakespeare makes fun of is told seriously in Chaucer's *Legend of Good Women*.

The Pyramus and Thisbe story is also found in the Roman poet Ovid's *Metamorphoses*, which Shakespeare knew in Arthur Golding's translation, first published in 1567. The name Titania (though not the character) comes from Ovid, too. Shakespeare took the name Oberon from the romance *Huon of Bordeaux* (published in the 1530s). The character of Puck comes from English folklore, as do the fairies.

Bottom and the other mechanicals are Shakespeare's own invention, though the idea that Bottom's head could be turned into that of an ass was

far from new. Again, Ovid's *Metamorphoses* was an inspiration to Shakespeare. It includes the story of King Midas, who is punished by being given an ass's ears. The classical story of Apuleius being turned into an ass was also well known at the time Shakespeare was writing: *The Golden Ass* had been translated by William Aldington in 1566 and ran to several editions, including one in 1596.

The plot

In four days' time, Theseus, Duke of Athens, will marry Hippolyta, Queen of the Amazons, whom he has conquered in battle. As he and his bride-to-be look forward happily to this event, the Duke is approached by Egeus, who asks for judgment on his daughter, Hermia. Egeus wants her to marry Demetrius, but she is in love with Lysander. Theseus rules that Hermia must either follow her father's will or choose between death and spending the rest of her life in a convent. She has four days to make up her mind.

Lysander and Hermia are left alone. He tells her that he has an aunt who lives beyond the boundaries of the Duke's power and suggests that they meet in the wood that night and run away so that they can marry. Hermia agrees. Hermia's friend Helena arrives. She is unhappy because she loves Demetrius, who does not return her love. Hermia and Lysander tell Helena of their plan to elope. She decides that she will tell Demetrius about it, hoping to gain his favor.

Meanwhile, a group of Athenian workmen—"mechanicals"—meet to prepare a play that they hope they will be invited to perform as part of the Duke's wedding festivities. Peter Quince, a carpenter, is nominally in charge, but the character of Bottom, a weaver, predominates. They decide to prepare a play telling the tragic story of the ill-fated lovers Pyramus and Thisbe. They are too stupid to realize how absurdly unsuited this story is to a happy occasion like a wedding. They decide which parts they are to play, and they agree to meet in the wood where they can rehearse in private.

The character Bottom in a 1986 Royal Opera House production.
Clive Barda/PAL

The fairies in a Regents Park Open Air Theatre production.
Fritz Curzon/PAL

Fairies live in the wood in which the mechanicals are to rehearse their play and in which Lysander and Hermia are to meet. Oberon and Titania, the fairy King and Queen, are quarreling. Titania will not allow Oberon to have the Indian orphan boy he has raised. Oberon wants the boy to be his page. He resolves to punish Titania and force her to give in; Oberon will cast a spell on her as she sleeps, so that she falls in love with the first creature she sees upon awakening.

Demetrius goes to the wood, too, searching for Hermia. Helena follows him, but he angrily rejects her. Oberon sees this, and he orders Puck to use the same magic on Demetrius that he has just used on Titania, so that Demetrius will return Helena's love. Oberon tells Puck that he will recognize the young Athenian by his clothing. Unfortunately, Puck comes across the other couple, Lysander and Hermia, and mistakenly applies the magic to Lysander. Helena

arrives and wakes up Lysander, and he falls instantly in love with her, spurning Hermia. Helena believes that Lysander is mocking her and runs away in tears. Hermia wakes up to find herself alone and goes off in search of Lysander.

Puck sees their absurd attempts at acting and decides to have some fun at their expense. He transforms Bottom's head into the head of an ass. Titania wakes up, sees Bottom, and falls in love with him.

Oberon discovers that Puck has mistakenly made Lysander fall in love with Helena. To correct the problem, he puts the love-juice on the sleeping Demetrius' eyes and orders Puck to bring Helena there. When Demetrius professes his love for her, Helena believes that Lysander and Demetrius are both teasing her. Hermia finds them, and Helena is convinced that she is in on the cruel joke, too. For her part, Hermia believes that Helena has stolen Lysander. The two men go off to fight to settle which of them shall have Helena, and she runs away from them all. Hermia is left alone and completely confused. Oberon orders Puck to separate Demetrius and Lysander and to arrange for all four young Athenians to fall asleep near each other. Puck then applies an antidote to Lysander.

Titania and Bottom fall asleep in each other's arms. Titania has meanwhile given Oberon the little Indian boy, so he releases her from the spell and they are reconciled to each other. Puck transforms Bottom's head back to normal.

Bottom and Titania in an Edinburgh production.
Clive Barda/PAL

Theseus, Hippolyta, and companions enter the wood. Theseus sees the four lovers asleep and orders them woken. Finding that they are now happily paired, Theseus orders that they should be allowed to wed as they choose, during his own marriage ceremony. Egeus' protests are dismissed.

After the triple wedding, the festivities include the performance of the story of Pyramus and Thisbe that the mechanicals have been preparing. The performance is comically absurd, but the wedding party is amused by it. The party ends at midnight, and the fairies appear, dance, and bless the union of the three couples.

Shakespearean comedy

We use the word *comedy* rather loosely these days to describe performances, movies, or TV programs that use various means to make us laugh. Certainly Shakespeare intended his audience to laugh at the plays we know as his comedies, and it is widely accepted that some of the scenes in *A Midsummer Night's Dream* are among the funniest ever written by anybody. But although Shakespeare's comedies contain many dramatic, verbal, and visual jokes, they are not just funny stories punctuated by gags.

Shakespeare included humor designed to appeal to the cultivated members of his audiences as well as the simple and uneducated, but he also offered his audiences something more than mere entertainment. That something was the opportunity to share in what is known as a "comic vision" of life. This means more than that life can be funny; it means that ultimately things turn out for the best. While we are watching the play, we can laugh at the things that go wrong because we know that we are in a world where they will certainly be put right.

This concept can be more easily understood if we compare *A Midsummer Night's Dream* with *Romeo and Juliet.* Each play begins with a family-frustrated love match and ends with the story of two lovers committing suicide because one of them mistakenly believes the other to be dead. (In Midsummer Night's Dream, the suicide is part of the play withing a play.) In *A Midsummer Night's Dream,* we are in a world—albeit a dream world—in which frustrated lovers find happiness against all the odds, and lovers' suicides can be laughed at because they are simply part of a badly told story. In *Romeo and Juliet*, we are in a world—and one that seems real enough while we are watching the play—in which genuine love is cruelly frustrated and lovers' suicides inspire desperate sadness. Such events have no place in a comic vision of life.

Key themes in *A Midsummer Night's Dream*

The dominant theme in *A Midsummer Night's Dream* is **love**, a subject to which Shakespeare returns constantly in his comedies. The play begins with a clear representation of the harmony between Theseus and Hippolyta, a love that matured after he conquered her in battle, and one that has reconciled the two former enemies. That love is very shortly to be sealed in **marriage**, another key theme of the play. The triple wedding at the end of Act IV marks the formal resolution of the romantic problems that have beset the two young couples from the beginning, when Egeus attempted to force his daughter to marry the man he had chosen to be her husband. The mature and stable love of Theseus and Hippolyta is contrasted with the relationship of Oberon and Titania, whose squabbling has such a negative impact on the world around them. Only when the marriage of the fairy King and Queen is put right can there be peace in their kingdom and the world beyond it. *A Midsummer Night's Dream* asserts marriage as the true fulfillment of romantic love. All the damaged relationships have been sorted out at the end of Act IV, and Act V serves to celebrate the whole idea of marriage in a spirit of festive happiness.

At one level, the story of the four young Athenians asserts that although "The course of true love never did run smooth," true love triumphs in the end, bringing happiness and harmony. At another level, however, the audience is forced to consider what an apparently irrational and whimsical thing love is, at least when experienced between youngsters. The recurrent association of love with sight, eyes, and blindness makes us wonder how such a powerful emotion can depend upon appearance. Ironically, the use of fairy magic to make people fall in and out of love with each other reminds us that real love itself is somehow magical, and often just as contrary to reason. At the same time that Shakespeare makes us laugh at what we do when we are (or think we are) in love, he invites us to wonder at the apparent illogicality of falling in love at all. Titania falls in love with the man-beast Bottom because she has had a magic spell cast upon her, but the play reminds us that people fall just as irrationally or inappropriately in love with each other without any need for external magic: Love has a magic of its own.

Another of the play's main themes is one to which Shakespeare returns again and again in his work: the difference between **appearance and reality**. The idea that things are not necessarily what they seem to be is at the heart of *A Midsummer Night's Dream*, and in the very title itself. A dream is not real, even though it seems so at the time we experience it. Shakespeare consciously creates the play's dreamlike quality in a number of ways. Characters frequently fall asleep and wake having dreamed

An Edinburgh production of A Midsummer Night's Dream.
Clive Barda/PAL

("Methought a serpent ate my heart away"); having had magic worked upon them so that they are in a dreamlike state; or thinking that they have dreamed ("I have had a dream, past the wit of man to say what dream it was"). Much of the play takes place at night, and there are frequent references to moonlight, which changes the appearance of what it illuminates.

That Shakespeare has created a dreamlike atmosphere on purpose is made clear in Puck's last speech, which is directly addressed to the audience:

> *If we shadows have offended,*
>
> *Think but this and all is mended:*
>
> *That you have but slumbered here*
>
> *While these visions did appear;*
>
> *And this weak and idle theme,*
>
> *No more yielding than a dream.*

Dreams, of course, are by definition unreal; but that does not mean that they are insignificant or that they cannot sometimes become true. If the members of the audience leave the theatre feeling that they have just woken up from a dream, they are still going to wonder what that dream signifies.

The difference between appearance and reality is also explored through the play-within-a-play, to particularly comic effect. The "rude mechanicals" completely fail to understand the magic of the theatre, which depends upon the audience being allowed to believe (for a time, at least) that what is being acted out in front of them is real. When Snug the Joiner tells the stage audience that he is not really a lion and that they must not be afraid of him, we (and they) laugh at his stupidity, but we also laugh at ourselves—for we know that he is not just a joiner pretending to be a lion, but an actor pretending to be a joiner pretending to be a lion. Shakespeare seems to be saying, "We all know that this play isn't real, but you're still sitting there and believing it." That is a kind of magic, too.

A Midsummer Night's Dream also deals with the theme of **order and disorder**. The order of Egeus' family is threatened because his daughter wishes to marry against his will; the social order of the state demands that a father's will should be enforced. When the city dwellers find themselves in the wood, away from their ordered and hierarchical society, order breaks down and relationships are fragmented. But this is a comedy, and relationships are more happily rebuilt in the free atmosphere of the wood before the characters return to society.

Natural order—the order of Nature—is also broken and restored in *A Midsummer Night's Dream*.

The Parthenon in Athens, which represents the order of society.
Gary Braasch/CORBIS

The row between the Fairy King and Queen results in the order of the seasons being disrupted:

The spring, the summer,

The chiding autumn, angry winter change

Their wonted liveries, and the mazèd world

By their increase knows not which is which.

Only after Oberon and Titania's reconciliation can all this be put right. Without the restoration of natural order, the happiness of the play's ending could not be complete.

Shakespeare's use of language: Imagery, verse, and prose

Shakespeare was not just a great playwright but a great poet, too, and a proper response to any of his plays takes this into account. Shakespeare chooses each word with a poet's care. It is important to appreciate not just *what* the characters say, but *how* they say it. The metaphors or similes they use and the images they put into our imagination affect the way we judge characters and events. By using images cumulatively, Shakespeare softens up our subconscious so that we are in the frame of mind he intentionally creates.

The dominant pattern of imagery in *A Midsummer Night's Dream* revolves around the moon and moonlight. The word *moon* occurs three times in the first nine lines of the play, the last of these three references in a most striking visual image: "the moon, like to a silver bow / New bent in heaven." One reason for repeating such images is to create the atmosphere of night. Shakespeare's plays were mostly performed by daylight, and he had to create the idea of darkness or half-light in the imagination of his audience—there were no lights to turn off or dim. In addition, these repeated moon references work upon the audience by creating a dreamlike atmosphere. Familiar things look different by moonlight; they are seen quite literally in a different light. The

moon itself is also a reminder of the passage of time, and that all things—like its phases—must change. The more educated people in Shakespeare's audience would also have understood the mythological significance of the moon. The moon-goddesses Luna and Diana were associated with chastity on the one hand and fertility on the other: two qualities that are united in faithful marriage, which the play celebrates.

Animal images also appear many times in the play, reminding us of the wildness of the woods in which most of the play's action takes place, where an unaccompanied female would be at "the mercy of wild beasts" in a setting where "the wolf behowls the moon." But this is a comedy; these dangers are not really threatening. The animal references are stylized and conventional. The only physical animals encountered by the characters (apart from Starveling's dog) are the less-than-half-ass Bottom and the totally artificial Lion played by Snug.

The animal references are included in the many images of the natural world that are associated with the fairy kingdom. These details emphasize the pretty delicacy of the fairies themselves and make the wood seem more real in the imagination of the audience. Oberon's "I know a bank" speech in Act II, Scene 1 is one of many fine examples of this.

A Midsummer Night's Dream also contains many references to seeing, eyes, and eyesight. These images serve a double purpose. The repetition reminds the audience of the difference between how things look and what they are (see the previous section), and that love is blind and beauty is in the eye of the beholder.

Most of Shakespeare's lines are written in blank or poetic verse, but at times he makes his characters speak in prose. When grand or noble characters change from verse to prose, the shift can mark a change in tone or mood from formal to informal, but common or lowlife characters tend to speak in prose as a matter of course. Prose is the normal mode of speech of the mechanicals, except when they recite the lines of their play, which are in poetic verse. The fact that their poetry is so comically bad emphasizes their lack of understanding and underlines that they are out of their depth.

Characters in the play

The characters in *A Midsummer Night's Dream* fall into four groups: the Athenian Court (The Duke, Hippolyta, Egeus, and Philostrate); the young lovers (Hermia, Lysander, Helena, and Demetrius); the fairy kingdom (Oberon, Titania, Puck, and the lesser fairies); and the Athenian workmen (Bottom, Quince, Flute, Snout, Starveling, and Snug). Though they are convincing in the context of the play, it would be wrong to judge any of these characters as if they were real human beings.

Theseus is a character from legend and is head of the Athenian state. His part in the play is to preside over Athens, maintaining order and justice. He is a model ruler—a type rather than a complex or rounded character—though he does display human qualities. Hippolyta is a legendary character, too, and does what is expected of her as a dutiful and obedient wife. She, too, is softened at the edges, showing sympathy to the young lovers and helping Moonshine out of his difficulties in the play-within-a-play. The individual characters of Theseus and Hippolyta, though, are less important than their collective function. Together, they demonstrate a type of mature and sensible love and a commitment to order and marriage.

Egeus is a one-dimensional character who performs the function of the inflexible father and who drops out of the plot at the end. Philostrate's part is short and undeveloped.

The young lovers are really more interesting as a group than as individuals. Their characters are confusingly similar, and purposely so. The point is that they are like all young lovers: quick to fall in and out of love and equally passionate in their expression of the extremeness of their emotions. Lysander and Demetrius each reject a girl they once loved; they fight first over one girl and then over the other. Hermia is short and Helena is tall, and there are some differences in their characters; Hermia is pluckier, for instance. But Shakespeare's interest is not as much in their individuality as in their similarity to one another. Like Lysander and Demetrius, they too are types.

Though Titania and Oberon are fairies, by definition unrealistic, what they show of their characters is strong and convincing. Oberon (like real human beings) has contradictory characteristics. He is resentful and spiteful to Titania when she refuses to hand over her boy, but he is sympathetic and generous in his attempts to make things

The four young lovers.
Fritz Curzon/PAL

go well for the young lovers. Titania is not one-sided, either. She stands up for herself strongly against Oberon, but she also shows very sensuous and gentle qualities in her deluded love for Bottom.

Puck, however, is neither complex nor realistic. He is a character straight from folklore and does what the folkloric Puck does: makes mischief. He would have been instantly recognized by Elizabethan audiences, and he behaves exactly as they would have expected him to, though Shakespeare adds the detail of making Puck the servant of Oberon, whose commands he obeys.

The Athenian workmen—the "rude mechanicals"—are quite unlike the other characters in the play, in that they are obviously drawn from life. They are not complex characters, though; they are like a collection of village idiots, whose dominating quality is stupidity. To that extent, they are caricatures. Strangely, though, the more foolishly they behave, the more sympathetically we regard them, because their idiocy is innocent, and they are only doing their best. Bottom's folly is compounded by his self-importance, but there is no malice in him. He is not only the star of the play-within-a-play, but in many ways the key character in *A Midsummer Night's Dream* itself. He is the only main character who is not paired off at the end of the play. When all the others are neatly married, they become less important as individuals than as partners. Bottom, however, is a comic creation that is unmatchable.

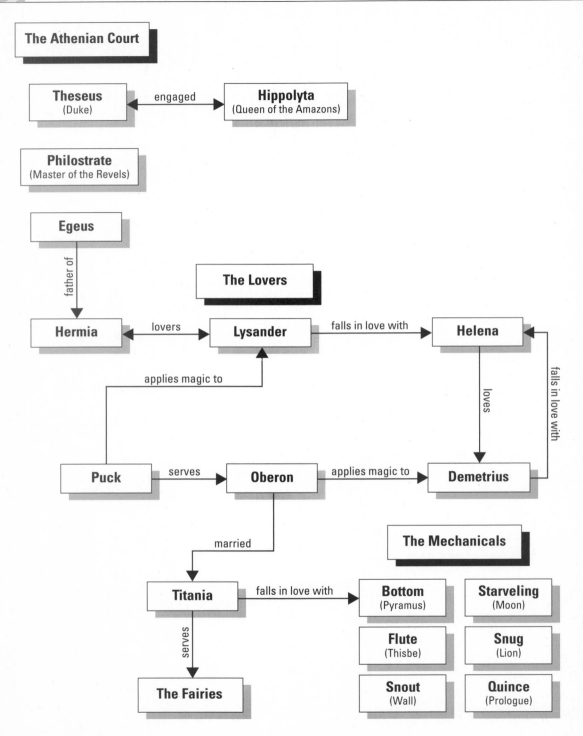

A MIDSUMMER NIGHT'S DREAM

ACT I

Hermia *If then true lovers have been ever crossed,*
It stands as an edict in destiny.
Then let us teach our trial patience,
Because it is a customary cross,
As due to love as thoughts, and dreams, and sighs,
Wishes and tears, poor fancy's followers.

Act I, Scene 1

The play begins in Athens. Theseus plans to marry Hippolyta. Hermia wants to marry Lysander, but is ordered to marry Demetrius, who is loved by Helena. Hermia and Lysander decide to run away together.

ACT I, SCENE 1

[Enter THESEUS, HIPPOLYTA, PHILOSTRATE, with others]

Theseus Now, fair Hippolyta, our nuptial hour
  Draws on apace; four happy days bring in
  Another moon; but, o, methinks, how slow
  This old moon wanes! She lingers my desires,
  Like to a step-dame or a dowager,   5
  Long withering out a young man's revenue.

Hippolyta Four days will quickly steep themselves in night;
  Four nights will quickly dream away the time;
  And then the moon, like to a silver bow
  New bent in heaven, shall behold the night   10
  Of our solemnities.

Theseus Go, Philostrate,
  Stir up the Athenian youth to merriments;
  Awake the pert and nimble spirit of mirth;
  Turn melancholy forth to funerals;
  The pale companion is not for our pomp.   15
  [Exit PHILOSTRATE]
  Hippolyta, I wooed thee with my sword,
  And won thy love doing thee injuries;
  But I will wed thee in another key,
  With pomp, with triumph, and with revelling.
  *[Enter EGEUS and his daughter HERMIA, and LYSANDER,
    and DEMETRIUS]*

Egeus Happy be Theseus, our renowned Duke!   20

Theseus Thanks, good Egeus. What's the news with thee?

NOTES

1. *nuptial:* marriage.

4. *lingers:* puts off.

5. *step-dame:* stepmother.
   dowager: widow.

6. *Long withering out a young man's revenue:* wasting a young man's inheritance.

7. *steep themselves:* soak themselves, be swallowed up in.

11. *solemnities:* formal celebrations.

14. *Turn melancholy forth:* banish sadness.

15. *companion:* a contemptuous term.

16. *wooed:* courted.

18. *key:* i.e., mood.

19. *pomp:* celebration.

Egeus Full of vexation come I, with complaint
Against my child, my daughter Hermia.
Stand forth, Demetrius!—My noble lord,
This man hath my consent to marry her.   25
Stand forth, Lysander!—And, my gracious Duke,
This man hath bewitched the bosom of my child.
Thou, thou, Lysander, thou hast given her rhymes,
And interchanged love-tokens with my child.
Thou hast by moonlight at her window sung   30
With feigning voice verses of feigning love,
And stolen the impression of her fantasy
With bracelets of thy hair, rings, gauds, conceits,
Knacks, trifles, nosegays, sweetmeats - messengers
Of strong prevailment in unhardened youth;   35
With cunning hast thou filched my daughter's heart;
Turned her obedience, which is due to me,
To stubborn harshness. And, my gracious Duke,
Be it so she will not here before your grace
Consent to marry with Demetrius,   40
I beg the ancient privilege of Athens;
As she is mine I may dispose of her;
Which shall be either to this gentleman
Or to her death, according to our law
Immediately provided in that case.   45

Theseus What say you, Hermia? Be advised, fair maid.
To you your father should be as a god,
One that composed your beauties; yea, and one
To whom you are but as a form in wax,
By him imprinted, and within his power   50
To leave the figure, or disfigure it.
Demetrius is a worthy gentleman.

Hermia So is Lysander.

Theseus In himself he is;
But, in this kind, wanting your father's voice,
The other must be held the worthier.   55

32. *And stolen the impression of her fantasy:* captured her imagination by making a secret impression of it.

33. *gauds:* showy trinkets.

     conceits: fancy things.

34. *Knacks:* knick-knacks.

35. *prevailment:* power to influence.

36. *filched:* stolen.

39. *Be it so:* if it turns out that.

45. *provided:* laid down (by law).

54. *in this kind, wanting your father's voice:* in this sort of case, lacking your father's approval.

Hermia I would my father looked but with my eyes.

Theseus Rather your eyes must with his judgment look.

Hermia I do entreat your grace to pardon me.
 I know not by what power I am made bold,
 Nor how it may concern my modesty   60
 In such a presence here to plead my thoughts:
 But I beseech your grace that I may know
 The worst that may befall me in this case
 If I refuse to wed Demetrius.

Theseus Either to die the death, or to abjure   65
 For ever the society of men.
 Therefore, fair Hermia, question your desires,
 Know of your youth, examine well your blood,
 Whether, if you yield not to your father's choice,
 You can endure the livery of a nun;   70
 For aye to be in shady cloister mewed,
 To live a barren sister all your life,
 Chanting faint hymns to the cold, fruitless moon.
 Thrice-blessèd they that master so their blood
 To undergo such maiden pilgrimage: 75
 But earthlier happy is the rose distilled
 Than that which, withering on the virgin thorn,
 Grows, lives, and dies, in single blessedness.

Hermia So will I grow, so live, so die, my lord,
 Ere I will yield my virgin patent up   80
 Unto his lordship, whose unwishèd yoke
 My soul consents not to give sovereignty.

Theseus Take time to pause; and by the next new moon,
 The sealing-day betwixt my love and me
 For everlasting bond of fellowship,   85
 Upon that day either prepare to die
 For disobedience to your father's will,
 Or else to wed Demetrius, as he would;
 Or on Diana's altar to protest
 For aye austerity and single life.   90

---

60. *concern:* be appropriate to.

68. *blood:* feelings.

70. *livery:* habit.

71. *aye:* ever.
    mewed: confined.

73. *fruitless:* barren.

76. *distilled:* (for perfume).

78. *single blessedness:* blessed state of being single.

80. *virgin patent:* right to my virginity.

89. *protest:* vow solemnly.

90. *aye:* ever.

Demetrius Relent, sweet Hermia; and, Lysander, yield
Thy crazèd title to my certain right.

Lysander You have her father's love, Demetrius;
Let me have Hermia's—do you marry him.

Egeus Scornful Lysander, true, he hath my love; 95
And what is mine my love shall render him;
And she is mine; and all my right of her
I do estate unto Demetrius.

Lysander I am, my lord, as well derived as he,
As well possessed; my love is more than his; 100
My fortunes every way as fairly ranked,
If not with vantage, as Demetrius';
And, which is more than all these boasts can be,
I am beloved of beauteous Hermia:
Why should not I then prosecute my right? 105
Demetrius, I'll avouch it to his head,
Made love to Nedar's daughter, Helena,
And won her soul; and she, sweet lady, dotes,
Devoutly dotes, dotes in idolatry,
Upon this spotted and inconstant man. 110

Theseus I must confess that I have heard so much,
And with Demetrius thought to have spoke thereof;
But, being over-full of self-affairs,
My mind did lose it. But, Demetrius, come;
And come, Egeus; you shall go with me; 115
I have some private schooling for you both.
For you, fair Hermia, look you arm yourself
To fit your fancies to your father's will,
Or else the law of Athens yields you up—
Which by no means we may extenuate— 120
To death, or to a vow of single life.
Come, my Hippolyta: what cheer, my love?
Demetrius, and Egeus, go along;
I must employ you in some business

92. *crazèd title:* flawed claim.

99. *as well derived:* of just as good a family.

100. *As well possessed:* equally wealthy.

102. *with vantage:* better.

106. *to his head:* to his face.

107. *Nedar's:* a name made up by Shakespeare.

110. *spotted:* (morally) blemished.

113. *over-full of self-affairs:* too busy with my own private concerns.

120. *extenuate:* mitigate.

122. *what cheer:* how are you?

124. *business:* (all three syllables are pronounced).

Against our nuptial, and confer with you　　　　　　　　　125
Of something nearly that concerns yourselves.

Egeus　With duty and desire we follow you.
[Exeunt all but Lysander and Hermia]

Lysander　How now, my love? Why is your cheek so pale?
How chance the roses there do fade so fast?

Hermia　Belike for want of rain, which I could well　　　130
Beteem them from the tempest of my eyes.

Lysander　Ay me! for aught that I could ever read,
Could ever hear by tale or history,
The course of true love never did run smooth:
But either it was different in blood—　　　　　　　　135

Hermia　O cross!—too high to be enthralled to low!

Lysander　Or else misgrafted in respect of years—

Hermia　O spite!—too old to be engaged to young!

Lysander　Or else it stood upon the choice of friends—

Hermia　O hell, to choose love by another's eyes!　　　140

Lysander　Or, if there were a sympathy in choice,
War, death, or sickness, did lay siege to it,
Making it momentany as a sound,
Swift as a shadow, short as any dream,
Brief as the lightning in the collied night　　　　　　145
That, in a spleen, unfolds both heaven and earth,
And ere a man hath power to say, 'Behold!'
The jaws of darkness do devour it up.
So quick bright things come to confusion.

Hermia　If then true lovers have been ever crossed,　　150
It stands as an edict in destiny.
Then let us teach our trial patience,
Because it is a customary cross,
As due to love as thoughts, and dreams, and sighs,
Wishes and tears, poor fancy's followers.　　　　　155

125.	*Against:* in preparation for.
130.	*Belike:* probably.
131.	*Beteem:* grant.
132.	*aught:* anything, all.
135.	*blood:* parentage.
141.	*sympathy:* agreement.
143.	*momentany:* momentary.
145.	*collied:* sooty, murky.
146.	*spleen:* fit of temper.
147.	*ere:* before.
150.	*crossed:* thwarted.

Lysander A good persuasion. Therefore, hear me, Hermia.
I have a widow aunt, a dowager
Of great revenue, and she hath no child.
From Athens is her house remote seven leagues;
And she respects me as her only son.   160
There, gentle Hermia, may I marry thee;
And to that place the sharp Athenian law
Cannot pursue us. If thou lov'st me then,
Steal forth thy father's house tomorrow night,
And in the wood, a league without the town,   165
Where I did meet thee once with Helena
To do observance to a morn of May,
There will I stay for thee.

Hermia My good Lysander!
I swear to thee by Cupid's strongest bow,
By his best arrow with the golden head,   170
By the simplicity of Venus' doves,
By that which knitteth souls and prospers loves,
And by that fire which burned the Carthage queen,
When the false Trojan under sail was seen,
By all the vows that ever men have broke—   175
In number more than ever women spoke—
In that same place thou hast appointed me,
Tomorrow truly will I meet with thee.

Lysander Keep promise, love. Look, here comes Helena.
[Enter HELENA]

Hermia God speed, fair Helena! Whither away?   180

Helena Call you me fair? That fair again unsay.
Demetrius loves your fair—O happy fair!
Your eyes are lodestars, and your tongue's sweet air
More tuneable than lark to shepherd's ear,
When wheat is green, when hawthorn buds appear.   185
Sickness is catching. O, were favour so,

157. *dowager:* widow.

158. *revenue:* (stressed on the second syllable).

159. *leagues:* A league is a measure of length equivalent to three miles.

168. *stay:* wait.

169. *Cupid's:* Cupid uses gold-tipped arrows to cause love and lead-tipped arrows for the opposite effect.

Cupid

171. *simplicity:* open honesty.

   Venus': Venus was the goddess of love.

172. *knitteth:* binds together.

173. *the Carthage queen:* Dido. In Virgil's *Aeneid,* she burns herself to death after Aeneas leaves her.

174. *false Trojan:* Aeneas.

182. *fair:* beauty.

183. *lodestars:* stars used (and thus gazed at) by navigators.

   air: tune.

186. *favour:* beauty.

Yours would I catch, fair Hermia, ere I go;
My ear should catch your voice, my eye your eye,
My tongue should catch your tongue's sweet melody.
Were the world mine, Demetrius being bated,   190
The rest I'd give to be to you translated.
O, teach me how you look, and with what art
You sway the motion of Demetrius' heart!

Hermia I frown upon him, yet he loves me still.

Helena O that your frowns would teach my smiles such skill! 195

Hermia I give him curses, yet he gives me love.

Helena O that my prayers could such affection move!

Hermia The more I hate, the more he follows me.

Helena The more I love, the more he hateth me.

Hermia His folly, Helena, is no fault of mine.   200

Helena None but your beauty; would that fault were mine!

Hermia Take comfort: he no more shall see my face;
Lysander and myself will fly this place.
Before the time I did Lysander see,
Seemed Athens as a paradise to me: 205
O, then, what graces in my love do dwell,
That he hath turned a heaven unto hell!

Lysander Helen, to you our minds we will unfold:
To-morrow night, when Phoebe doth behold
Her silver visage in the watery glass,   210
Decking with liquid pearl the bladed grass,
A time that lovers' flights doth still conceal,
Through Athens' gates have we devised to steal.

190.   *bated:* excepted.

191.   *translated:* transformed.

209.   *Phoebe:* another name for Diana, the moon-goddess.

210.   *visage:* face.

212.   *still:* invariably.

Hermia And in the wood where often you and I
Upon faint primrose beds were wont to lie,   215
Emptying our bosoms of their counsel sweet,
There my Lysander and myself shall meet:
And thence from Athens turn away our eyes,
To seek new friends and stranger companies.
Farewell, sweet playfellow. Pray thou for us,   220
And good luck grant thee thy Demetrius!
Keep word, Lysander. We must starve our sight
From lovers' food, till morrow deep midnight.

Lysander I will, my Hermia.
[Exit HERMIA]

Lysander Helena, adieu:
As you on him, Demetrius dote on you!   225
[Exit LYSANDER]

Helena How happy some o'er other some can be!
Through Athens I am thought as fair as she.
But what of that? Demetrius thinks not so;
He will not know what all but he do know.
And as he errs, doting on Hermia's eyes,   230
So I, admiring of his qualities.
Things base and vile, holding no quantity,
Love can transpose to form and dignity.
Love looks not with the eyes, but with the mind;
And therefore is winged Cupid painted blind.   235
Nor hath love's mind of any judgment taste;
Wings and no eyes figure unheedy haste:
And therefore is love said to be a child,
Because in choice he is so oft beguiled.
As waggish boys in game themselves forswear,   240
So the boy Love is perjured everywhere.
For ere Demetrius looked on Hermia's eyne,
He hailed down oaths that he was only mine;
And when this hail some heat from Hermia felt,
So he dissolved, and showers of oaths did melt.   245
I will go tell him of fair Hermia's flight;

215. *faint:* pale.

219. *stranger companies:* the companionship of strangers.

226. *How happy some o'er other some can be!:* How much happier are some people than others!

232. *holding no quantity:* having no relation to the value that love puts on them.

235. *Cupid:* In paintings, Cupid was often represented as being blind.

237. *figure:* symbolize.

239. *beguiled:* deceived.

240. *waggish:* mischievous.

in game themselves forswear: swear falsely in games.

242. *ere:* before.

eyne: eyes.

245. *oaths:* solemn promises.

Then to the wood will he to-morrow night
Pursue her; and for this intelligence
If I have thanks, it is a dear expense;
But herein mean I to enrich my pain,   250
To have his sight thither and back again.
[Exit]

248.   *intelligence:* information.

249.   *a dear expense:* a great sacrifice.

COMMENTARY

The scene is ancient Athens, though the time and place are not especially significant, because this is a fairy story and is effectively set "once upon a time, in a faraway place." In four days, Theseus, the Duke of Athens, will marry Hippolyta, Queen of the Amazons, whom he conquered in battle. He is impatient: "but, o, methinks, how slow / This old moon wanes! She lingers my desires." Hippolyta tells him that the time will pass quickly, saying that soon "the moon, like to a silver bow / Now bent in heaven, shall behold the night / Of our solemnities."

Each character speaks of time measured by the phases of the moon. The word *moon* occurs three times in the play's first ten lines and is referred to many times later in the play. This repetition is significant: Mentions of the moon remind the audience that most of the play (though not, perhaps, this scene) takes place at night, and moonlight has a magical, dream-like quality that makes everything look different. Educated members of Shakespeare's audience would also have associated the moon with the Roman goddess of chastity, Luna—a reminder that this is a play in which characters must wait (until marriage) for sexual fulfillment.

Theseus sends Philostrate to get the city prepared for the grand wedding, and Egeus arrives with his daughter, Hermia, along with Lysander and Demetrius. He has come "Full of vexation" to the Duke for judgment on Hermia. She refuses to marry Demetrius (the man Egeus has chosen for her

husband) because she is in love with Lysander. From the start, Shakespeare makes clear that the two young men are remarkably similar, and many productions of the play emphasize this by casting actors of a similar appearance to play their parts. But despite their similarities in appearance, background, or wealth, Hermia loves one of them totally and cannot love the other. Unfortunately, as far as her father is concerned, she loves the wrong one. According to the law of Athens, Hermia's options are to marry the man of her father's choice, be put to death, or become a nun, "Chanting faint hymns to the cold, fruitless moon." A nun's life is described as sterile, solitary, and without warmth; a nun is a "barren sister" who lives a "single life" of "austerity" in a "shady cloister." This life is a harsh contrast with the love and companionship that Hermia yearns for. Theseus judges that she must make up her mind before his own wedding, which is only four days off.

Shakespeare establishes in this scene that the next four days will be crucial in the lives of the main characters we have met. The time-scale he sets establishes a sense of urgency and pace: The word *four* is used three times in the first eight lines. In fact, a close reading of the text reveals that Shakespeare was so keen to keep up the pace that the action of the play is completed in only two days and one night. Some critics see this as a mistake, though if it is, it is certainly not noticed by the audience when the play is performed.

Hermia and Lysander are left alone, and Lysander suggests that they should elope. He has an aunt who lives beyond the area governed by the laws of Athens: They can go to stay with her and get married. They agree to meet in a nearby wood the next evening and then make their escape. (The wood, like the woods and forests in several of Shakespeare's other plays, is a place where the rules and structures of civilized life don't operate, and in which relationships can be shaken up, changed, or healed.)

Hermia's friend Helena appears. Helena is heart-broken because she is in love with Demetrius, who had returned her love until he fell for Hermia. Lysander tells Helena that he and Hermia are going to run away together. Helena decides that she will tell Demetrius, so that he will follow them into the wood, where Helena thinks she might be able to win him back.

The language of the first scene is formal and highly stylized. The characters are all grand or noble, and Shakespeare marks this by making them speak in *blank verse*, unrhymed lines of iambic pentameter. (See the Introduction for an explanation of iambic pentameter.) Theseus and Hippolyta speak grandly, as befits their rank. Their words are balanced, structured, and rhetorical, like well-crafted public speeches. Balance and contrast is characteristic of the speeches of the other characters in this scene, too—qualities that emphasize the similarity between Lysander and Demetrius and the difficult choice that Hermia must make.

Egeus speaks formally, but his language, unlike the speech of Theseus and Hippolyta, is cold and cynical. His speeches are full of "I"s, "me"s, and "my"s; indeed, he refers to Hermia as "my child" as if she were his possession, to do with as he

chooses. He dismisses Lysander's expressions of love for Hermia as tricks, but the list of deceits that he then catalogues sound just like the things that young people give each other when they are genuinely in love. An example of Shakespeare's use of contrast in this scene is in the language of Egeus' accusations against Lysander. He accuses him of having given Hermia "bracelets of thy hair, rings, gauds, conceits, / Knacks, trifles, nosegays, sweetmeats" and the like—items that are innocent in themselves but by which Lysander has wickedly "filched" Hermia's heart and "stolen the impression of her fantasy."

Shakespeare's audience would have been sympathetic to the convention that a woman should marry for duty and would perhaps have nodded at Theseus' statement to Hermia that "To you your father should be as a god." But his audience would also have known how hard this duty can be. The harshness and coldness of Egeus' tone—"As she is mine I may dispose of her"—would put them at least partly on his daughter's side. He comes across as a stuffy and unsympathetic character and is separated from all the other people in the play by his age. He seems to have forgotten what it is like to be young.

Helena and Hermia speak to each other by echoing, repeating, and reversing each other's words and phrases. Hermia says of Demetrius, "I frown upon him, yet he loves me still." Helena picks up the phrases and returns them: "O that your frowns would teach my smiles such skill." This emphasizes their similarities and underlines their friendship at the same time as highlighting their contrasting fortunes in love.

When Lysander and Hermia are alone toward the end of the scene, they speak to each other in the kind of language that Shakespeare's audience would recognize as conventional for young lovers. Lysander refers to Hermia's cheeks as having lost their roses in her sadness; she picks up his image by saying that she could water those roses abundantly with the tears she has wept. They speak of their feelings and their circumstances in extreme terms, and they lament the fact that "The course of true love never did run smooth." Hermia's promise to meet Lysander is given in rhyming couplets, as is nearly all of the remainder of the scene. This poetic shift intensifies the expression of the lovers' feelings, but it also somehow ritualizes it and reminds us that this is, after all, a play—and a comedy, too.

Helena's closing speech of the scene is a soliloquy, because all the other characters have left. It contains some extremely important observations on the nature of love, which leave the audience thinking—as she does—that love is blind as well as irrational: "Love looks not with the eyes, but with the mind; / And therefore is winged Cupid painted blind. / Nor hath love's mind of any judgment taste." The audience will later realize that it is no coincidence that the magic used to change people's affections is poured into their eyes.

Act I, Scene 2

Another part of Athens. Quince, Snug, Bottom, Flute, Snout, and Starveling plan to stage a play for the Duke's wedding feast.

ACT I, SCENE 2

[Enter QUINCE the Carpenter, and SNUG the Joiner, and
  BOTTOM the Weaver, and FLUTE the Bellows-mender, and
  SNOUT the Tinker and STARVELING the Tailor]

Quince Is all our company here?

Bottom You were best to call them generally, man by man,
  according to the scrip.

Quince Here is the scroll of every man's name which is
  thought fit through all Athens to play in our   5
  interlude before the Duke and the Duchess on
  his wedding-day at night.

Bottom First, good Peter Quince, say what the play treats
  on; then read the names of the actors; and so
  grow to a point.   10

Quince Marry, our play is 'The most lamentable comedy and
  most
  cruel death of Pyramus and Thisbe'.

Bottom A very good piece of work, I assure you, and a merry.
  Now, good Peter Quince, call forth your   15
  actors by the scroll. Masters, spread yourselves.

Quince Answer as I call you. Nick Bottom, the weaver?

Bottom Ready. Name what part I am for, and proceed.   20

NOTES

2. *generally:* Bottom uses the wrong word; he means "individually."

3. *scrip:* another mistake: Bottom means "script."

8. *treats on:* deals with, is about.

10. *grow to a point:* come to a conclusion.

13. *Pyramus and Thisbe:* doomed lovers whose story is told in Ovid's collection of poems, *Metamorphoses.*

16. *spread yourselves:* spread out.

Quince　You, Nick Bottom, are set down for Pyramus.

Bottom　What is Pyramus? A lover or a tyrant?

Quince　A lover that kills himself most gallantly for love.　25

Bottom　That will ask some tears in the true performing
of it. If I do it, let the audience look to their
eyes: I will move storms; I will condole in some
measure. To the rest—yet my chief humour is　30
for a tyrant: I could play Ercles rarely, or a part
to tear a cat in, to make all split:
The raging rocks
And shivering shocks
Shall break the locks　35
　Of prison gates,
And Phibbus' car
Shall shine from far,
And make and mar
　The foolish Fates.　40
This was lofty. Now name the rest of the players.
This is Ercles' vein, a tyrant's vein; a lover
is more condoling.

Quince　Francis Flute, the bellows-mender?

Flute　Here, Peter Quince.　45

Quince　Flute, you must take Thisbe on you.

Flute　What is Thisbe? A wandering knight?

Quince　It is the lady that Pyramus must love.

Flute　Nay, faith, let not me play a woman; I have a
beard coming.　50

Quince　That's all one; you shall play it in a mask, and
you may speak as small as you will.

26.　*ask:* require.

29.　*condole:* express grief.

31.　*Ercles:* a bad pronunciation of *Hercules,* the hero of classical mythology.

Hercules

32.　*tear a cat:* rant and bluster.

37.　*Phibbus':* a bad pronunciation of Phoebus, the sun god.

　　　car: chariot.

42.　*vein:* style.

52.　*small:* thin, high-pitched.

Bottom An I may hide my face, let me play Thisbe too.
I'll speak in a monstrous little voice;'Thisne,
Thisne!'—'Ah, Pyramus, my lover dear; thy   55
Thisbe dear! and lady dear!'

Quince No, no, you must play Pyramus; and, Flute,
you Thisbe.

Bottom Well, proceed.

Quince Robin Starveling, the tailor?   60

Starveling Here, Peter Quince.

Quince Robin Starveling, you must play Thisbe's
mother. Tom Snout, the tinker?

Snout Here, Peter Quince.

Quince You, Pyramus' father; myself, Thisbe's father;   65
Snug, the joiner, you, the lion's part; and, I hope,
here is a play fitted.

Snug Have you the lion's part written? Pray you, if it
be, give it me, for I am slow of study.

Quince You may do it extempore, for it is nothing but   70
roaring.

Bottom Let me play the lion too: I will roar that I will
do any man's heart good to hear me; I will roar
that I will make the Duke say 'Let him roar again,
let him roar again!'   75

Quince An you should do it too terribly, you
would fright the Duchess and the ladies, that they
would shriek; and that were enough to hang us
all.

53. *An:* if.

70. *extempore:* off the cuff.

All That would hang us, every mother's son.   80

Bottom I grant you, friends, if you should fright the
ladies out of their wits, they would have no more
discretion but to hang us; but I will aggravate
my voice so, that I will roar you as gently as
any sucking dove; I will roar you an 'twere any   85
nightingale.

Quince You can play no part but Pyramus; for Pyramus
is a sweet-faced man; a proper man, as one shall
see in a summer's day; a most lovely gentleman-
like man; therefore you must needs play   90
Pyramus.

Bottom Well, I will undertake it. What beard were I best
to play it in?

Quince Why, what you will.

Bottom I will discharge it in either your straw-colour   95
beard, your orange-tawny beard, your purple-in-
grain beard, or your French-crown-colour
beard, your perfect yellow.

Quince Some of your French crowns have no hair at
all, and then you will play bare-faced. But, mas-   100
ters, here are your parts, and I am to entreat you,
request you, and desire you, to con them by to-
morrow night; and meet me in the palace wood,
a mile without the town, by moonlight; there
will we rehearse: for if we meet in the city, we   105
shall be dogged with company, and our devices
known. In the meantime I will draw a bill of
properties, such as our play wants. I pray you,
fail me not.

83. *aggravate:* a malapropism for "moderate."

84. *you:* for you.

85. *sucking dove:* another mistake: Bottom confuses a "sitting dove" and a "sucking lamb."

an 'twere: as if it were.

90. *needs:* necessarily.

96. *orange-tawny:* tan-colored.

purple-in-grain: fast-dyed scarlet or crimson.

97. *French-crown-colour:* the colour of French gold coins.

99. *French crowns:* a reference to the baldness caused by syphilis, "the French disease."

102. *con:* learn.

107. *draw a bill:* draw up a list.

Bottom We will meet; and there we may rehearse most
Obscenely and courageously. Take pains; be
perfect; adieu!   110

Quince At the Duke's oak we meet.

Bottom Enough; hold, or cut bow-strings.

[Exeunt]

111.   *Obscenely:* another mistake, perhaps for "seemly."

114.   *hold, or cut bow-strings:* (obscure) perhaps, "if we don't stick to this plan, we'd might just as well give up."

COMMENTARY

There is an instant change of atmosphere, from the elevated and intense to the hilarious and ridiculous. The "mechanicals"—workmen—arrive, and their conversation is in prose, a convention that Shakespeare uses to mark their lowly status, differentiating them from the grander characters introduced earlier. Their language is down-to-earth and un-poetic, and Bottom's is riddled with comic blunders and malapropisms (clumsily mistaken vocabulary). Bottom begins by suggesting that Quince calls the company "generally," when what he must mean is 'individually'; later, he says he can "aggravate" his voice when he means he can 'moderate' it. The mechanicals clearly have very few brains between them. Flute does not recognize the name of the famous heroine of their play, and thinks she might be a "wandering knight." Snug admits that he is "slow of study", and fears he won't be able to learn his lines. Quince—who is in charge of the group—has enough sense to know Snug's limitations, for he has chosen the part of the lion for him: the lion does not speak, it only roars. Quince also cleverly persuades Bottom to take the part of Pyramus by extravagantly describing the character as full of virtues, and this is irresistibly appealing to Bottom's vanity. But it is Quince who sets the tone of absurdity which characterizes everything the mechanicals do or say, when he announces the nonsensical title of the play he has chosen for them: "'The most lamentable comedy and most cruel death of Pyramus and Thisbe.'" The idea of a "lamentable comedy" is a contradiction in terms. A comedy can have tragic elements, or *vice versa*: 'tragi-comedy' is a genre in its own right. Straight tragedies often include comic scenes for light relief. The 'Porter's Scene' in Shakespeare's *Macbeth* is a classic example. But the particular phrase "lamentable comedy" suggests a comedy that fails to work as a comedy because it is so bad. The full title of the mechanicals' play is also a parody (see Introduction for explanation of this term) of some of the over-blown play titles of Shakespeare's time, which included phrases such as 'lamentable tragedy' and 'new tragical comedy.'

The names of the mechanicals underline their characters or trades, and are quite unlike the exotic names of the other characters in the play. There is nothing Athenian about them: They are thoroughly Elizabethan workmen. The name "Quince" is suggestive of the word 'quoins'—the wedges used by carpenters; "Snug" suggests the close fitting expertise of joinery; "Flute" suggests the high-pitched voice of an actor used to playing female parts; "Snout" puts one in mind of the nozzles and spouts on the kettles and pans that would be mended by a tinker. Tailors were proverbially

The mechanicals in an Edinburgh production of A Midsummer Night's Dream.
Clive Barda/PAL.

learns that he is down to play Pyramus, he assumes that it must be a grand and important part, that of a "lover or a tyrant." When he learns that it is indeed a "lover that kills himself most gallantly for love," he boasts that he will move the audience to tears, and launches into a speech in which he shows off his acting ability—and in which Shakespeare parodies the puffed-up poetic style of some earlier playwrights. At the end of the speech, Bottom congratulates himself on it—"This was lofty"—before anyone else has a chance to comment. Lofty it may have been, but it contains one of Bottom's many verbal clumsinesses: he calls the sun god "Phibbus" instead of 'Phoebus.' As the other mechanicals are given their parts, it is clear that Bottom wants to play all the best ones. He demonstrates that he can do a "monstrous little voice" for Thisbe, and says that if he is given the part of the lion he will roar so that the Duke will demand an encore of his roaring. When Quince and the others express the fear that this might upset the ladies in the audience and get the actors into trouble, he absurdly promises that he would roar "as gently as any sucking dove." He is clearly a loveable fool; later, he will be foolishly loved, to highly comic effect.

skinny and feeble; hence, "Starveling." A 'bottom' of thread was a term used by a weaver. By giving the mechanicals such definitive names as these, Shakespeare makes it clear that they are uncomplicated characters and establishes them as figures of fun.

Though Peter Quince is in charge of the production of the 'play within a play,' the story of the mechanicals is dominated by Bottom, whose character is much more developed than those of the others. His ludicrous self-importance is offset by his energy and childish enthusiasm. He interrupts Quince immediately, telling him how he should be doing his job: "You were best to call them generally, man by man, according to the scrip." Quince is in charge of the players, but Bottom behaves as if he were in charge of Quince. As soon as Bottom

NOTES

NOTES

NOTES

NOTES

NOTES

A MIDSUMMER NIGHT'S DREAM
ACT II

Oberon *Having once this juice,*
I'll watch Titania when she is asleep,
And drop the liquor of it in her eyes:
The next thing then she waking looks upon—
Be it on lion, bear, or wolf, or bull,
On meddling monkey, or on busy ape—
She shall pursue it with the soul of love.

Act II, Scene 1

A wood near Athens. Oberon plans to force Titania to give him her little Indian prince by magic. He will make her fall in love with whatever creature she first sees upon waking, and only release her when she obeys him. Oberon overhears Helena pleading with Demetrius, and tells Puck to use the same magic to make Demetrius love Helena.

ACT II, SCENE 1

		NOTES
[*Enter a FAIRY at one door, and ROBIN GOODFELLOW at another*]		
Puck How now, spirit: whither wander you?		
Fairy Over hill, over dale,		
Thorough bush, thorough brier,		4. *Thorough:* through.
Over park, over pale,	5	5. *park:* parkland.
Thorough flood, thorough fire,		*pale:* fence.
I do wander everywhere,		
Swifter than the moon's sphere;		
And I serve the fairy queen,		
To dew her orbs upon the green.		9. *orbs:* circles; fairy rings.
The cowslips tall her pensioners be:	10	10. *pensioners:* members of the royal bodyguard.
In their gold coats spots you see;		
Those be rubies, fairy favours,		
In those freckles live their savours;		13. *savours:* scents.
I must go seek some dew-drops here,		
And hang a pearl in every cowslip's ear.	15	
Farewell, thou lob of spirits; I'll be gone.		16. *lob:* clumsy fool.
Our queen and all her elves come here anon.		
Puck The king doth keep his revels here to-night;		
Take heed the Queen come not within his sight.		
For Oberon is passing fell and wrath,	20	20. *passing fell and wrath:* exceedingly fierce and angry.
Because that she as her attendant hath		
A lovely boy, stol'n from an Indian king;		
She never had so sweet a changeling;		23. *changeling:* an ugly child exchanged for a beautiful one by fairies.
And jealous Oberon would have the child		
Knight of his train, to trace the forests wild:	25	25. *trace:* range over.
But she perforce withholds the lovèd boy,		
Crowns him with flowers, and makes him all her joy.		

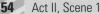

And now they never meet in grove or green,
By fountain clear, or spangled starlight sheen,
But they do square, that all their elves for fear   30
Creep into acorn cups, and hide them there.

Fairy Either I mistake your shape and making quite,
Or else you are that shrewd and knavish sprite
Called Robin Goodfellow. Are not you he
That frights the maidens of the villagery,   35
Skim milk, and sometimes labour in the quern,
And bootless make the breathless housewife churn;
And sometime make the drink to bear no barm;
Mislead night-wanderers, laughing at their harm?
Those that Hobgoblin call you, and sweet Puck,   40
You do their work, and they shall have good luck:
Are not you he?

Puck Thou speak'st aright;
I am that merry wanderer of the night.
I jest to Oberon, and make him smile,
When I a fat and bean-fed horse beguile,   45
Neighing in likeness of a filly foal;
And sometime lurk I in a gossip's bowl,
In very likeness of a roasted crab;
And, when she drinks, against her lips I bob,
And on her withered dewlap pour the ale.   50
The wisest aunt, telling the saddest tale,
Sometime for three-foot stool mistaketh me;
Then slip I from her bum, down topples she,
And 'tailor' cries, and falls into a cough;
And then the whole choir hold their hips and laugh,   55
And waxen in their mirth, and neeze, and swear
A merrier hour was never wasted there.
But room, fairy, here comes Oberon.

Fairy And here my mistress. Would that he were gone!

---

30. *square:* argue.

33. *sprite:* fairy.

36. *Skim:* i.e., steal the cream from.
quern: mill for grinding corn by hand.

37. *bootless:* in vain.
churn: make butter.

38. *barm:* yeast.

45. *bean-fed:* i.e., well-fed.

47. *gossip's:* chatterer's.

48. *crab:* crab apple.

50. *dewlap:* hanging fold of skin at the throat.

51. *aunt:* old woman.

54. *'tailor':* (obscure) a word called out when one falls over.

55. *choir:* company.

56. *waxen:* wax, grow.
neeze: sneeze.

58. *room:* give me room, stand aside.

[*Enter OBERON, the King of the Fairies at one door, with his Train; and TITANIA, the Queen, at another, with hers*]

Oberon   Ill met by moonlight, proud Titania.   60

Titania   What, jealous Oberon? Fairies, skip hence;
I have forsworn his bed and company.

Oberon   Tarry, rash wanton! Am not I thy lord?

Titania   Then I must be thy lady; but I know
When thou hast stol'n away from fairy-land,   65
And in the shape of Corin sat all day,
Playing on pipes of corn, and versing love
To amorous Phillida. Why art thou here,
Come from the farthest step of India,
But that, forsooth, the bouncing Amazon,   70
Your buskined mistress and your warrior love,
To Theseus must be wedded, and you come
To give their bed joy and prosperity?

Oberon   How canst thou thus, for shame, Titania,
Glance at my credit with Hippolyta,   75
Knowing I know thy love to Theseus?
Didst not thou lead him through the glimmering night
From Perigenia, whom he ravishèd?
And make him with fair Aegles break his faith,
With Ariadne and Antiopa?   80

Titania   These are the forgeries of jealousy:
And never, since the middle summer's spring,
Met we on hill, in dale, forest, or mead,
By pavèd fountain, or by rushy brook,
Or on the beachèd margent of the sea,   85
To dance our ringlets to the whistling wind,
But with thy brawls thou hast disturbed our sport.
Therefore the winds, piping to us in vain,
As in revenge, have sucked up from the sea
Contagious fogs; which, falling in the land,   90
Hath every pelting river made so proud
That they have overborne their continents:

62.	*forsworn:* renounced.
63.	*wanton:* (1) rebellious, spoiled child (2) slut.
66.	*Corin:* typical name for shepherd.
67.	*pipes of corn:* musical instruments made of corn straws.
68.	*Phillida:* typical name for shepherdess.
69.	*step:* limit.
70.	*forsooth:* in truth.
	Amazon: legendary female warrior.
71.	*buskined:* booted.
75.	*Glance at:* allude to critically.
78–80.	*Perigenia . . . Aegles . . . Ariadne . . . Antiopa:* (legend) women loved and abandoned by Theseus.
82.	*the middle summer's spring:* i.e., the beginning of mid-summer.
83.	*mead:* meadow.
85.	*margent:* margin.
86.	*ringlets:* circular dances (that would leave 'fairy rings' behind).
87.	*brawls:* (1) clamour (2) rough dances.
90.	*Contagious:* disease-bearing.
91.	*pelting:* paltry.
92.	*overborne their continents:* burst their banks.

The ox hath therefore stretched his yoke in vain,
The ploughman lost his sweat; and the green corn
Hath rotted ere his youth attained a beard. 95
The fold stands empty in the drownèd field,
And crows are fatted with the murrion flock;
The nine men's morris is filled up with mud,
And the quaint mazes in the wanton green
For lack of tread are undistinguishable: 100
The human mortals want their winter here;
No night is now with hymn or carol blest:
Therefore the moon, the governess of floods,
Pale in her anger, washes all the air,
That rheumatic diseases do abound: 105
And thorough this distemperature we see
The seasons alter: hoary-headed frosts
Fall in the fresh lap of the crimson rose;
And on old Hiems' chin and icy crown
An odorous chaplet of sweet summer buds 110
Is, as in mockery, set. The spring, the summer,
The childing autumn, angry winter, change
Their wonted liveries; and the mazed world,
By their increase, now knows not which is which:
And this same progeny of evils comes 115
From our debate, from our dissension:
We are their parents and original.

Oberon Do you amend it, then: it lies in you.
Why should Titania cross her Oberon?
I do but beg a little changeling boy 120
To be my henchman.

Titania Set your heart at rest;
The fairy-land buys not the child of me.
His mother was a vot'ress of my order:
And, in the spicèd Indian air, by night,
Full often hath she gossiped by my side, 125
And sat with me on Neptune's yellow sands,

---

94. *lost:* i.e., wasted.

97. *murrion:* infected with disease (of sheep).

98. *nine men's morris:* (grooves in the ground made for) an outdoor game something like checkers.

99. *quaint:* intricate.

wanton green: lush grass.

105. *rheumatic:* causing discharges (as do colds).

106. *thorough:* through.

distemperature: disorder in nature.

109. *Hiems:* Winter, personified as an old man.

110. *chaplet:* wreath.

112. *childing:* fruitful, productive.

113. *wonted:* accustomed.

liveries: dress.

mazed: bewildered.

114. *increase:* produce.

116. *debate:* quarrel.

117. *original:* origin.

120. *but:* only.

121. *henchman:* squire, page.

123. *vot'ress:* woman who has taken (nun's) vows.

126. *Neptune's:* Roman god of the seas.

Marking th' embarkèd traders on the flood;
When we have laughed to see the sails conceive
And grow big-bellied with the wanton wind;
Which she, with pretty and with swimming gait   130
Following, her womb then rich with my young squire,
Would imitate, and sail upon the land,
To fetch me trifles, and return again
As from a voyage, rich with merchandise.
But she, being mortal, of that boy did die;   135
And for her sake do I rear up her boy;
And for her sake I will not part with him.

Oberon How long within this wood intend you stay?

Titania Perchance till after Theseus' wedding-day.
If you will patiently dance in our round,   140
And see our moonlight revels, go with us.
If not, shun me, and I will spare your haunts.

Oberon Give me that boy and I will go with thee.

Titania Not for thy fairy kingdom. Fairies, away:
We shall chide downright if I longer stay.   145
[Exit TITANIA and her Train]

Oberon Well, go thy way: thou shalt not from this grove
Till I torment thee for this injury.
My gentle Puck, come hither: thou rememb'rest
Since once I sat upon a promontory,
And heard a mermaid, on a dolphin's back   150
Uttering such dulcet and harmonious breath
That the rude sea grew civil at her song
And certain stars shot madly from their spheres
To hear the sea-maid's music.

Puck I remember.

Oberon That very time I saw, but thou couldst not, 155
Flying between the cold moon and the earth,
Cupid, all armed: a certain aim he took

127.   *traders:* merchant ships.

Neptune

139.   *Perchance:* perhaps.

142.   *spare:* avoid.

145.   *chide:* argue.

149.   *Since:* when.

152.   *rude:* (1) uncivil (2) rough.

153.   *spheres:* orbits.

At a fair vestal, thronèd by the west,

And loosed his love-shaft smartly from his bow

As it should pierce a hundred thousand hearts;   160

But I might see young Cupid's fiery shaft

Quenched in the chaste beams of the watery moon;

And the imperial vot'ress passèd on,

In maiden meditation, fancy-free.

Yet marked I where the bolt of Cupid fell: 165

It fell upon a little western flower,

Before milk-white; now purple with love's wound,

And maidens call it 'love-in-idleness'.

Fetch me that flower, the herb I showed thee once;

The juice of it on sleeping eyelids laid   170

Will make or man or woman madly dote

Upon the next live creature that it sees.

Fetch me this herb, and be thou here again

Ere the leviathan can swim a league.

Puck   I'll put a girdle round about the earth   175

In forty minutes!

[Exit]

Oberon   Having once this juice,

I'll watch Titania when she is asleep,

And drop the liquor of it in her eyes:

The next thing then she waking looks upon—

Be it on lion, bear, or wolf, or bull,   180

On meddling monkey, or on busy ape—

She shall pursue it with the soul of love.

And ere I take this charm from off her sight—

As I can take it with another herb—

I'll make her render up her page to me.   185

But who comes here? I am invisible,

And I will overhear their conference.

[Enter DEMETRIUS, HELENA following him]

Demetrius   I love thee not, therefore pursue me not.

Where is Lysander and fair Hermia?

---

158.   *vestal:* vestal virgin.

    by: in the region of.

163.   *imperial:* imperious.

165.   *bolt:* arrow.

167.   *purple:* i.e., of the color of blood.

168.   *'love-in-idleness':* the pansy.

174.   *leviathan:* giant sea-monster.

The one I'll slay, the other slayeth me.   190
Thou told'st me they were stol'n into this wood,
And here am I, and wood within this wood,
Because I cannot meet with Hermia.
Hence, get thee gone, and follow me no more.

Helena You draw me, you hard-hearted adamant!   195
But yet you draw not iron, for my heart
Is true as steel. Leave you your power to draw,
And I shall have no power to follow you.

Demetrius Do I entice you? Do I speak you fair?
Or, rather, do I not in plainest truth   200
Tell you I do not, nor I cannot love you?

Helena And even for that do I love you the more.
I am your spaniel; and, Demetrius,
The more you beat me, I will fawn on you:
Use me but as your spaniel, spurn me, strike me,   205
Neglect me, lose me; only give me leave,
Unworthy as I am, to follow you.
What worser place can I beg in your love—
And yet a place of high respect with me—
Than to be used as you use your dog?   210

Demetrius Tempt not too much the hatred of my spirit;
For I am sick when I do look on thee.

Helena And I am sick when I look not on you.

Demetrius You do impeach your modesty too much,
To leave the city, and commit yourself   215
Into the hands of one that loves you not;
To trust the opportunity of night,
And the ill counsel of a desert place,
With the rich worth of your virginity.

Helena Your virtue is my privilege, for that.   220
It is not night when I do see your face,

192. *wood:* frantic (a pun).

194. *Hence:* Get away.

195. *draw:* attract me (like a magnet).

adamant: (1) magnet (2) extremely hard substance.

214. *impeach:* call in doubt.

220. *privilege:* guarantee of immunity.

Therefore I think I am not in the night;
Nor doth this wood lack worlds of company,
For you, in my respect, are all the world.
Then how can it be said I am alone   225
When all the world is here to look on me?

Demetrius I'll run from thee, and hide me in the brakes,   **227.**   *brakes:* thickets.
And leave thee to the mercy of wild beasts.

Helena The wildest hath not such a heart as you.
Run when you will, the story shall be changed;   230
Apollo flies, and Daphne holds the chase;   **231.**   *Apollo:* sun god.
The dove pursues the griffin; the mild hind   *Daphne:* nymph who was turned into
Makes speed to catch the tiger—bootless speed,   a laurel when running away from
When cowardice pursues and valour flies.   Apollo.

Demetrius I will not stay thy questions. Let me go;   235   **232.**   *griffin:* mythical creature with the
Or, if thou follow me, do not believe   head and wings of an eagle and the
But I shall do thee mischief in the wood.   body of a lion.

                                                                              hind: female deer.

Helena Ay, in the temple, in the town, the field,   **233.**   *bootless:* useless.
You do me mischief. Fie, Demetrius!
Your wrongs do set a scandal on my sex.   240   **240.**   *Your wrongs do set a scandal on my
We cannot fight for love as men may do;   sex:* You force me to act in a scan-
We should be wooed, and were not made to woo.   dalously unladylike fashion.
[Exit DEMETRIUS]
I'll follow thee, and make a heaven of hell,
To die upon the hand I love so well.   **244.**   *upon:* by means of.
[Exit]

Oberon Fare thee well, nymph. Ere he do leave this grove,   245   **245.**   *nymph:* wood-dwelling maid.
Thou shalt fly him, and he shall seek thy love.
[Enter PUCK]
Hast thou the flower there? Welcome, wanderer.

Puck Ay, there it is.

Oberon I pray thee give it me.
I know a bank whereon the wild thyme blows,
Where oxlips and the nodding violet grows;   250   **250.**   *oxlips:* hybrid of cowslip and primrose.
Quite over-canopied with luscious woodbine,   **251.**   *woodbine:* convolvulus (bindweed).

With sweet musk-roses, and with eglantine:
There sleeps Titania sometime of the night,
Lulled in these flowers with dances and delight;
And there the snake throws her enamelled skin, 255
Weed wide enough to wrap a fairy in;
And with the juice of this I'll streak her eyes,
And make her full of hateful fantasies.
Take thou some of it, and seek through this grove:
A sweet Athenian lady is in love 260
With a disdainful youth. Anoint his eyes;
But do it when the next thing he espies
May be the lady. Thou shalt know the man
By the Athenian garments he hath on.
Effect it with some care, that he may prove 265
More fond on her than she upon her love.
And look thou meet me ere the first cock crow.

Puck Fear not, my lord; your servant shall do so.
[Exeunt]

252. *musk-roses:* wild, fragrant roses.

eglantine: sweetbriar (a type of wild rose).

255. *throws:* casts off.

256. *Weed:* clothing.

266. *fond on:* in love with.

COMMENTARY

Another change of atmosphere and language: We now encounter the world of the fairy kingdom. Puck asks the Fairy where it is going, and it answers him in rhyming verse, with a speech that evokes the magical atmosphere in which it operates: it is going about the countryside at night, leaving fairy rings, and decorating flowers with dewdrops. It tells Puck that Titania will come there that evening. He points out that Oberon is coming, too, which is unfortunate, as the royal pair have been unable to meet without arguing ever since Titania refused to give him the orphaned Indian boy she has brought up.

The images that occur in the speeches of Puck and the Fairy come from nature: they speak of flowers, forests, and fountains that are their habitat. Shakespeare's exquisite use of language makes these natural features seem not just real to our imaginations, but magically beautiful. The Fairy describes cowslips (wild flowers) as Titania's "pensioners," an image that brings to mind the grandly dressed royal bodyguard of the real Queen of England, Elizabeth the First. The freckles on their flowers become "rubies" decorating their coats, and drops of dew become their earrings—all put there by fairies. This personification is not only one of the compliments to Queen Elizabeth that Shakespeare pays in *A Midsummer Night's Dream*, it is a good example of how he associates his fairies with the idea of royalty in general. His fairy world is a kingdom; its king, queen, and subjects bless the real world with their touch, or blight it when they are at odds with each other.

Shakespeare's audience would have been familiar with the idea of fairies, and stories about them were told not just for children, but for adults—even if not everyone believed them. Fairy folklore is one of the sources Shakespeare uses for the play, and (as ever) he turns his source material into something new and special. So successfully has he done this in *A Midsummer Night's Dream* that when people have subsequently thought of, written about, or drawn pictures of fairies, it is the creatures of this play that have usually come to mind. This is particularly true of the character of Puck, although strictly speaking he is not a fairy, but a 'hobgoblin.' When nowadays people use the word 'Puckish,' meaning 'having a mischievous sense of humour,' they think of Shakespeare's character in the *Dream*, although the folklore character Puck (or 'Pook') existed long before Shakespeare re-created him. Shakespeare's audience would have instantly recognized the character.

Puck is introduced very precisely. The Fairy gives a detailed description of him, which Puck then confirms and elaborates. He is also known as 'Robin Goodfellow,' notoriously responsible for those things in life that go wrong without any apparent reason. When milk won't turn to butter, when beer making fails, or when people get lost in the dark, as often as not it is Puck who is to blame. It amuses him to make old women spill their drink or fall off their stools, and he performs such tricks for the amusement of Oberon, his master.

Oberon and Titania meet, and the mood becomes suddenly somber. Puck and the Fairy have spoken in rhymed couplets; the Fairy King and Queen address each other in blank verse, using grand language to convey the intensity and pride of their feelings. They fall instantly to arguing. To Oberon, Titania is "proud;" to Titania, Oberon is "jealous." She accuses him of having had an affair with Hippolyta; he accuses her of loving Theseus. Their quarrelling is one of the problems that will need to be resolved if the play is to end happily. Moreover, their disharmony is causing disruption in the natural world. The weather has been unseasonal: "The spring, the summer, / The chiding autumn, angry winter, change / Their wonted liveries; and the mazed world, / By their increase, now knows not which is which." In a detail that reminds us that Shakespeare's countryside in *A Midsummer Night's Dream* is thoroughly English and sixteenth century, Oberon points out that the mazes and patterns cut in the turf for the traditional country game of "nine men's morris" have been flooded. Worse, people and animals are sick, rivers have burst their banks, crops have rotted in the fields, and summer flowers have been killed by unseasonal frosts—all because of the quarrelling between the Fairy King and Queen. Oberon says that all this can be put right if only Titania would give him the little changeling boy, which she refuses to do at any price. She had adopted him after the death of his mother, who had been one of her most devoted followers. She will not part with him "for her sake." She leaves before the quarrel can get worse, and Oberon resolves to punish her and force her to give up the child by means of magic. He orders Puck to fetch him the herb known as 'love-in-idleness,' describing how it came to have its powers: at a magical moment in the past, one of Cupid's arrows had fallen on it. He will put its juice in Titania's sleeping eyes, which will make her fall in love with whichever creature she first sees when she awakes. He will only release the spell when she gives up the boy. Demetrius and Helena now appear, and Oberon makes himself invisible so that he can watch them. (Elizabethan actors conveyed 'invisibility' by wrapping themselves in a large cloak.) Demetrius and Helena are also at odds. Demetrius is furious that Helena is pursuing him; she says that the more he spurns her, the more she loves him. Oberon and Titania have quarreled grandly and proudly, as a king and queen might, but these two ordinary young lovers speak of more intimate feelings. Demetrius is mad ("wood") for love of Hermia; Helena is drawn to him as if by a magnet. Her love for him is pitifully painful. "I am your spaniel," she says to him. "The more you beat me, I will fawn on you." He, however, is made furious by her pleading, saying "I am sick when I do look on thee." She replies "And I am sick when I look not on you," one of many occasions in the play when a statement is reversed and thrown back to the person who makes it. This pattern underlines one of Shakespeare's purposes in the play, which is to emphasize that love is absolute: people are either absolutely in love, or absolutely not. Similarly, the characters often mention opposites in their speeches, as in Helena's "I'll follow thee, and make a heaven of hell." (Placing such opposite ideas closely together like this is called 'antithesis'.) There is no room (or time) for half-measures in *A Midsummer Night's Dream*.

Oberon takes pity on Helena, thinking her "A sweet Athenian lady," and he wants to make things right for her. His gentle sympathy contrasts directly with the rage he has just shown to his wife. When Puck returns with the magic herb, he orders him to use it to make Demetrius fall in love with Helena.

He tells Puck he will recognize him by his Athenian garments, and this later turns out to be poor advice. Meanwhile, Oberon will apply the magic to Titania, who is sleeping on a bank that is described in what have become some of Shakespeare's most famous lines. Blank verse gives way to rhyming couplets, and the rhythm emphasizes the atmosphere of the magic that has just been mentioned. The language appeals to all five senses: sight, touch, taste, smell, and hearing. What the place *looks* like is described in exquisite detail: in their imagination, the audience can see the violets nod, and Shakespeare's choice of the word "enamelled" makes the brightness of the snakeskin instantly vivid. The *feel* of the place—what it would be like to be in physical contact with it—is suggested by the idea of a fairy being wrapped in the snakeskin. *Taste* and *smell are* appealed to in the word that describes the heavily scented woodbine, "luscious." The soothing *sounds* of the setting are conveyed by the repeated hard and soft 's' sounds in the passage, as in "oxlips" (hard 's', twice) and "musk-roses" (hard followed by two softs). It is in passages like this that Shakespeare uses his own, real magic—the power to make something seem real in our imaginations through poetry.

The scene ends with another reminder that time is moving fast. Oberon is ordered to return "ere the first cock crow."

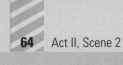

Act II, Scene 2

Another part of the wood. Oberon puts the magic juice in Titania's eyes. Puck puts it in Lysander's, mistaking him for Demetrius. Lysander wakes, and falls in love with Helena.

ACT II, SCENE 2

[Enter TITANIA, Queen of the Fairies, with her Train]

Titania Come, now a roundel and a fairy song,
Then, for the third part of a minute, hence:
Some to kill cankers in the musk-rose buds,
Some war with reremice for their leathern wings,
To make my small elves coats, and some keep back   5
The clamorous owl, that nightly hoots and wonders
At our quaint spirits. Sing me now asleep;
Then to your offices, and let me rest.
[FAIRIES sing]

First Fairy You spotted snakes, with double tongue,
Thorny hedgehogs, be not seen;   10
   Newts and blindworms do no wrong;
Come not near our Fairy Queen.

Chorus Philomel, with melody,
   Sing in our sweet lullaby:
Lulla, lulla, lullaby; lulla, lulla, lullaby: 15
   Never harm
   Nor spell, nor charm,
   Come our lovely lady nigh.
   So good-night, with lullaby.

Second Fairy Weaving spiders, come not here;   20
   Hence, you long-legged spinners, hence;
 Beetles black, approach not near;
   Worm nor snail do no offence.

Chorus Philomel with melody, &c.
[TITANIA sleeps]

NOTES

1. *roundel:* round dance.

3. *cankers:* canker worms, caterpillars.

4. *reremice:* bats.

7. *quaint:* dainty.

8. *offices:* duties.

11. *blindworms:* slow-worms.

13. *Philomel:* the nightingale.

First Fairy Hence away; now all is well.   25
One, aloof, stand sentinel.
*[Exeunt FAIRIES. Enter OBERON. He drops the juice on
   TITANIA'S eyelids]*

Oberon What thou seest when thou dost wake,
Do it for thy true love take;
Love and languish for his sake.
Be it ounce, or cat, or bear,   30
Pard, or boar with bristled hair,
In thy eye that shall appear
When thou wak'st, it is thy dear;
Wake when some vile thing is near.
[Exit]
[Enter LYSANDER and HERMIA]

Lysander Fair love, you faint with wandering in the wood,   35
And, to speak troth, I have forgot our way.
We'll rest us, Hermia, if you think it good,
And tarry for the comfort of the day.

Hermia Be it so, Lysander: find you out a bed,
For I upon this bank will rest my head.   40

Lysander One turf shall serve as pillow for us both;
One heart, one bed, two bosoms, and one troth.

Hermia Nay, good Lysander; for my sake, my dear,
Lie farther off yet, do not lie so near.

Lysander O, take the sense, sweet, of my innocence;   45
Love takes the meaning in love's conference.
I mean that my heart unto yours is knit;
So that but one heart we can make of it:
Two bosoms interchainèd with an oath;
So then two bosoms and a single troth.   50
Then by your side no bed-room me deny;
For lying so, Hermia, I do not lie.

30. *ounce:* lynx.

31. *Pard:* leopard.

36. *troth:* truth.

46. *conference:* conversation.

Hermia Lysander riddles very prettily:
  Now much beshrew my manners and my pride
  If Hermia meant to say Lysander lied.   55
  But, gentle friend, for love and courtesy
  Lie further off, in human modesty.
  Such separation as may well be said
  Becomes a virtuous bachelor and a maid:
  So far be distant; and good night, sweet friend: 60
  Thy love ne'er alter till thy sweet life end!

Lysander Amen, amen, to that fair prayer say I;
  And then end life when I end loyalty!
  Here is my bed: Sleep give thee all his rest!

Hermia With half that wish the wisher's eyes be pressed!   65
[They sleep]
[Enter PUCK]

Puck Through the forest have I gone,
  But Athenian found I none,
  On whose eyes I might approve
  This flower's force in stirring love.
  Night and silence—Who is here?   70
  Weeds of Athens he doth wear:
  This is he, my master said,
  Despisèd the Athenian maid;
  And here the maiden, sleeping sound
  On the dank and dirty ground.   75
  Pretty soul, she durst not lie
  Near this lack-love, this kill-courtesy.
  Churl, upon thy eyes I throw
  All the power this charm doth owe.
[He drops the juice on LYSANDER'S eyelids]
  When thou wak'st let love forbid   80
  Sleep his seat on thy eyelid:
  So, awake when I am gone;
  For I must now to Oberon.
[Exit]
[Enter DEMETRIUS and HELENA, running]

54. *much beshrew:* a curse upon.

59. *Becomes:* suits.

68. *approve:* put to the test.

71. *Weeds:* clothing.

79. *owe:* own, possess.

Helena Stay, though thou kill me, sweet Demetrius.

Demetrius I charge thee, hence, and do not haunt me thus.　85

Helena O, wilt thou darkling leave me? Do not so.

Demetrius. Stay on thy peril; I alone will go.
  [Exit]

Helena O, I am out of breath in this fond chase!
  The more my prayer, the lesser is my grace.
  Happy is Hermia, wheresoe'er she lies,　90
  For she hath blessèd and attractive eyes.
  How came her eyes so bright? Not with salt tears—
  If so, my eyes are oftener washed than hers.
  No, no, I am as ugly as a bear;
  For beasts that meet me run away for fear:　95
  Therefore no marvel though Demetrius
  Do, as a monster, fly my presence thus.
  What wicked and dissembling glass of mine
  Made me compare with Hermia's sphery eyne?
  But who is here? Lysander, on the ground?　100
  Dead, or asleep? I see no blood, no wound.
  Lysander, if you live, good sir, awake.

Lysander *[Waking]* And run through fire I will for thy sweet
  sake.
  Transparent Helena! Nature shows art,
  That through thy bosom makes me see thy heart.　105
  Where is Demetrius? O, how fit a word
  Is that vile name to perish on my sword!

Helena Do not say so, Lysander; say not so.
  What though he love your Hermia? Lord, what though?
  Yet Hermia still loves you; then be content.　110

Lysander Content with Hermia? No, I do repent
  The tedious minutes I with her have spent.

85.　*I charge thee hence:* I order you to get away.

86.　*darkling:* in the dark.

88.　*fond:* foolish.

89.　*The more my prayer, the lesser is my grace:* The harder I pray, the less my prayer is answered.

98.　*glass:* looking-glass, mirror.

99.　*sphery eyne:* eyes like stars (in their spheres).

104.　*Transparent:* (1) able to be seen through (2) open.

109.　*what though:* what does it matter if.

Not Hermia but Helena I love.
Who will not change a raven for a dove?
The will of man is by his reason swayed; 115
And reason says you are the worthier maid.
Things growing are not ripe until their season;
So I, being young, till now ripe not to reason;
And touching now the point of human skill,
Reason becomes the marshal to my will, 120
And leads me to your eyes, where I o'erlook
Love's stories, written in love's richest book.

Helena Wherefore was I to this keen mockery born?
When at your hands did I deserve this scorn?
Is't not enough, is't not enough, young man, 125
That I did never—no, nor never can—
Deserve a sweet look from Demetrius' eye,
But you must flout my insufficiency?
Good troth, you do me wrong, good sooth, you do
In such disdainful manner me to woo. 130
But fare you well. Perforce I must confess,
I thought you lord of more true gentleness.
O, that a lady of one man refused
Should of another therefore be abused!
[Exit]

Lysander She sees not Hermia. Hermia, sleep thou there, 135
And never mayst thou come Lysander near.
For, as a surfeit of the sweetest things
The deepest loathing to the stomach brings,
Or as the heresies that men do leave
Are hated most of those they did deceive, 140
So thou, my surfeit and my heresy,
Of all be hated, but the most of me!
And, all my powers, address your love and might
To honour Helen, and to be her knight!
[Exit]

118. *ripe:* ripened.

119. *point:* height, highest point.
  skill: discrimination.

120. *marshal:* official in charge (at a banquet).

121. *o'erlook:* read through.

123. *Wherefore:* why.

131. *Perforce:* of necessity.

132. *gentleness:* gentlemanliness.

133. *of one:* by one.

139–140. *as the heresies that men do leave . . . deceive:* just as men hate heresies that once deceived them.

Hermia *[Waking]* Help me, Lysander, help me! Do thy best   145
To pluck this crawling serpent from my breast!
Ay me, for pity! What a dream was here!
Lysander, look how I do quake with fear!
Methought a serpent ate my heart away,
And you sat smiling at his cruel prey.   150
Lysander! What, removed? Lysander! Lord!
What, out of hearing? Gone? No sound, no word?
Alack, where are you? Speak, an if you hear;
Speak, of all loves! I swoon almost with fear.
No? Then I well perceive you are not nigh: 155
Either death or you I'll find immediately.
[Exit]

COMMENTARY

The action continues from the previous scene without interruption. Titania orders her fairies to sing her to sleep and then to get on with their duties: killing the canker worms that destroy the beauty of roses, fending off owls, and collecting bats' wings to make coats for her elves. That they can achieve such things in a mere 20 seconds ("the third part of a minute") emphasizes the speed at which fairies operate. Their speed, and the tininess of their tasks, underlines the minute scale of their world.

The fairies sing, and Titania sleeps. Oberon appears and squeezes the magic juice onto her eyelids. Before Titania wakes, Lysander and Hermia appear on another part of the stage. When Lysander suggests that they should lie down and sleep side by side, Hermia suggests that "in human modesty" they should sleep a decent distance apart. Puck enters and sees Lysander lying asleep but does not notice Hermia. Seeing that Lysander is wearing the Athenian garments that Oberon has said will identify Demetrius, Puck mistakenly squeezes the juice in Lysander's eyes. After Puck

leaves, Helena and Demetrius run onto the stage. Demetrius has not been able to shake off Helena so far, but she is now "out of breath," and he makes his escape. Helena notices Lysander lying asleep and wakes him up, and he falls instantly in love with her. When he professes his love, Helena assumes that he is mocking her, and she leaves. Lysander pursues her. Hermia wakes, having had a nightmare. She dreamed that a serpent had eaten away her heart. She sees that Lysander is gone and runs off to look for him.

Shakespeare uses a variety of speech patterns in this scene, each generating a particular effect. Titania's speech at the beginning is written in blank verse, but the rest of the scene is constructed in various sorts of rhyme. This change intensifies the mood of magic in the fairy kingdom. The song is a lullaby, such as a mother might sing to send her baby to sleep. This suggests an affectionate bond between Titania and her fairy servants and shows that there is a gentle side to the Fairy Queen's character as well as the authoritative and haughty side she has shown in her argument with Oberon.

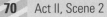

Oberon and Titania in an Edinburgh production.
Clive Barda/PAL

Another contrast in language appears within the song itself. The chorus is soft and soothing, sweetly appealing to the nightingale to add its beautiful voice to the lullaby. But the verses contain dark and ugly images, listing the ominous creepy crawlies from which Titania is to be defended: snakes, spiders, newts, hedgehogs, worms, snails, and beetles. (Such creatures are all small—there are no large snakes in England—and this again reminds us of the tininess of the fairies.) The fairies' prayer that no "harm / Nor spell, nor charm, / Come our lovely lady nigh" is an example of dramatic irony, a device in which the audience knows what the characters don't. What the fairies don't know is that when Titania falls asleep, Oberon is going to do exactly what they believe their song will prevent: put a spell on her.

The song slows the play's action to a momentary stop: Titania sleeps. Oberon then administers the magic juice accompanied by rhyming couplets

appropriate for a solemn spell or charm. The dialogue between Lysander and Hermia that follows is also rhymed, but the lines are constructed in pentameters, and the rhythm reflects the poise and balance of their love for each other. Lysander's attempts to persuade Hermia to let him lie down beside her are balanced by Hermia's confident but affectionate insistence that they should sleep at a decent distance. When they say good night, Hermia offers the wish that sleep should be impressed upon Lysander's eyes. The irony of Hermia's wish is that magic will soon be impressed upon Lysander's eyes, and it will play havoc with these two lovers.

Puck's speech makes a dramatic contrast with the lovers' dialogue. Its shorter lines echo the rhythm of Oberon's lines when administering the juice to Titania's eyes, reminding us that Puck and Oberon are creatures from the fairy, not the human, world. After Puck's exit, Helena and Demetrius run onto the stage, and their brief exchange of speeches is in single lines, each uttering a line which is completed by the other to make a rhyming couplet. There is not even a pause for breath in their exchanges. Their argument speeds up the pace for a moment or two. Demetrius leaves.

The scene's pace slows again during Helena's soliloquy, in which she laments the fact that nobody now loves her. She mentions eyes four times in the speech. Hermia, she says, is lucky because her eyes are attractive. But eyes are for seeing, as well as being seen. Helena feels that when she looked at her own eyes in a mirror, she was deceived into thinking that they were as pretty as Hermia's. She now believes she is so ugly that even wild animals run away from her.

The repeated reference to eyes in Helena's speech is important. Eye images are used frequently in *A Midsummer Night's Dream*, reminding us of one of Shakespeare's recurrent interests: the difference between appearance and reality, between what things look like and what they actually are. The central theme of this play is love, and people tend to fall in love with those who appear beautiful to them. People we think we love at one time in our lives can later seem not only unattractive but even repellent. For a time, this attraction to beauty might *appear* to be love at its most intense, but one of the ideas of the play is that *real* love is much more than mere physical attraction.

When Lysander wakes, the pace quickens again as he expresses the love for Helena that Puck's magic has caused him to feel. His instant and absolute rejection of his previous love for Hermia is one of the many sudden swings and reversals in the play, which together leave the audience wondering what makes people fall in and out of love so completely in real life. Lysander now says that the time he previously spent with Hermia was "tedious" and suggests that she was like a "raven" (black and ugly) compared to Helena, who is like a "dove" (white and beautiful). Lysander justifies his love by explaining that it is reasonable. This is as comic as it is ironic, for the audience knows it has actually come about by the application of magic. The hatred he expresses for the sleeping Hermia is even more unreasonable, and the scene ends with her waking from a prophetic dream to find Lysander gone without knowing why or where.

NOTES

NOTES

NOTES

NOTES

NOTES

CLIFFSCOMPLETE

A MIDSUMMER NIGHT'S DREAM

ACT III

Bottom *Not a whit. I have a device to make all well. Write me a prologue; and let the prologue seem to say we will do no harm with our swords, and that Pyramus is not killed indeed; and for the more better assurance, tell them that I Pyramus am not Pyramus, but Bottom the weaver: this will put them out of fear.*

Act III, Scene 1

As the clowns rehearse their play, the mischievous Puck tranforms Bottom's head into the head of an ass. Titania, who has been sleeping nearby, wakes, sees Bottom, and falls in love with him.

ACT III, SCENE I

[Enter the Clowns: QUINCE, SNUG, BOTTOM, FLUTE, SNOUT, and STARVELING]

Bottom Are we all met?

Quince Pat, pat; and here's a marvellous convenient place for our rehearsal. This green plot shall be our stage, this hawthorn brake our tiring-house, and we will do it in action, as we will do it be-   5
fore the Duke.

Bottom Peter Quince,

Quince What sayest thou, bully Bottom?

Bottom There are things in this comedy of 'Pyramus and Thisbe' that will never please. First, Pyramus   10
must draw a sword to kill himself, which the ladies cannot abide. How answer you that?

Snout By'r lakin, a parlous fear!

Starveling I believe we must leave the killing out, when all is done.   15

Bottom Not a whit. I have a device to make all well. Write me a prologue; and let the prologue seem to say we will do no harm with our swords, and that Pyramus is not killed indeed; and for the   20
more better assurance, tell them that I Pyramus am not Pyramus, but Bottom the weaver: this will put them out of fear.

NOTES

2.   *pat:* punctually.

4.   *brake:* thicket.
     tiring-house: dressing room.

8.   *bully:* fine fellow.

14.   *By'r lakin:* By Our Lady—a light oath, made lighter by the use of the contracted diminutive form of lady, 'ladykin'.
     parlous: perilous.

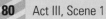

Quince Well, we will have such a prologue; and it shall be
written in eight and six.   25

Bottom No, make it two more; let it be written in
eight and eight.

Snout Will not the ladies be afeard of the lion?

Starveling I fear it, I promise you.

Bottom Masters, you ought to consider with yourselves   30
to bring in—God shield us!—a lion among ladies
is a most dreadful thing: for there is not a more
fearful wildfowl than your lion living; and we
ought to look to't.

Snout Therefore another prologue must tell he is not a lion.   35

Bottom Nay, you must name his name, and half his face
must be seen through the lion's neck, and he
himself must speak through, saying thus, or to
the same defect, 'Ladies', or 'Fair ladies, I would   40
wish you', or 'I would request you', or, 'I would
entreat you, not to fear, not to tremble: my life
for yours. If you think I come hither as a lion, it
were pity of my life. No, I am no such thing; I am
a man as other men are'—and there, indeed, let   45
him name his name, and tell them plainly he is
 Snug the joiner.

Quince Well, it shall be so. But there is two hard things;
That is, to bring the moonlight into a chamber—
for, you know, Pyramus and Thisbe meet by   50
moonlight.

Snug Doth the moon shine that night we play our
play?

---

25. *in eight and six:* alternating lines of eight and six syllables (ballad meter).

26. *in eight and eight:* each line with eight syllables.

33. *wildfowl:* another of Bottom's verbal mistakes.

Bottom A calendar, a calendar! Look in the almanack—
find out moonshine, find out moonshine!　　　　　　　55

Quince Yes, it doth shine that night.

Bottom Why, then may you leave a casement of the
great chamber window where we play open,
and the moon may shine in at the casement.

Quince Ay, or else one must come in with a bush of
thorns and a lantern, and say he comes to dis-　　　60
figure or to present the person of moonshine.
Then there is another thing: we must have a
wall in the great chamber; for Pyramus and
Thisbe, says the story, did talk through the　　　65
chink of a wall.

Snout You can never bring in a wall. What say you,
Bottom?

Bottom Some man or other must present Wall; and let him have
some plaster, or some loam, or some　　　　　　70
rough-cast about him, to signify wall; and let
him hold his fingers thus, and through that
cranny shall Pyramus and Thisbe whisper.

Quince If that may be, then all is well. Come, sit down,
Every mother's son, and rehearse your parts.　　　75
Pyramus, you begin: when you have spoken
your speech, enter into that brake; and so every
one according to his cue.
[Enter PUCK behind]

Puck What hempen homespuns have we swaggering here,
So near the cradle of the Fairy Queen?　　　　　80
What, a play toward! I'll be an auditor—
An actor too perhaps, if I see cause.

54. *almanack:* calendar of astronomical and other events, including phases of the moon.

70. *loam:* mixture of sand, clay, and straw.

71. *rough-cast:* lime and gravel mix.

72. *fingers thus:* the fingers straight and together, except for one parting.

79. *hempen homespuns:* roughly-dressed characters (wearing homemade clothes of coarse material).

81. *auditor:* listener, member of audience.

Quince Speak, Pyramus. Thisbe, stand forth.

Bottom *(as Pyramus)* Thisbe, the flowers of odious savours sweet

Quince Odours, odours.   85

Bottom *(as Pyramus)* . . . odours savours sweet:
So hath thy breath, my dearest Thisbe dear.
But hark, a voice! Stay thou but here awhile,
And by and by I will to thee appear.
[Exit]

Puck A stranger Pyramus than e'er played here!   90
[Exit]

Flute Must I speak now?

Quince Ay, marry, must you: for you must understand
he goes but to see a noise that he heard, and is to
come again.

Flute *(as Thisbe)* Most radiant Pyramus, most lily white of hue,   95
Of colour like the red rose on triumphant briar,
    Most brisky juvenal, and eke most lovely Jew,
As true as truest horse, that would never tire,
    I'll meet thee, Pyramus, at Ninny's tomb—

Quince 'Ninus' tomb', man! Why, you must not speak   100
that yet; that you answer to Pyramus. You speak
all your part at once, cues, and all. Pyramus enter: your cue is past; it is 'never tire.'

Flute O— *(as Thisbe)* As true as truest horse, that yet would
never tire.   105
[Enter PUCK, and BOTTOM with the ass head on]

Bottom *(as Pyramus)* If I were fair, fair Thisbe, I were only thine.

Quince O monstrous! O strange! We are haunted.

84.	*odious:* another of Bottom's malapropisms.
89.	*by and by:* in a little while.
92.	*marry:* by (the Virgin) Mary—a light oath.
96.	*triumphant:* magnificent.
97.	*brisky juvenal:* lively juvenile.
	eke: also.
	Jew: Flute's misreading of "jewel," perhaps.
99.	*Ninny's:* fool's.

Pray, masters! Fly, masters! Help!
*[Exeunt QUINCE, SNUG, FLUTE, SNOUT, and
    STARVELING]*

Puck I'll follow you; I'll lead you about a round,
Through bog, through bush, through brake, through briar;   110
    Sometime a horse I'll be, sometime a hound,
A hog, a headless bear, sometime a fire;
    And neigh, and bark, and grunt, and roar, and burn,
Like horse, hound, hog, bear, fire, at every turn.
[Exit]

Bottom Why do they run away? This is a knavery of   115
them to make me afeard.
[Enter SNOUT]

Snout O Bottom, thou art changed! What do I see on thee?

Bottom What do you see? You see an ass-head of your
own, do you?   120
[Re-enter QUINCE]

Quince Bless thee, Bottom, bless thee! Thou art translated!
[Exit]

Bottom I see their knavery: this is to make an ass of
me; to fright me, if they could. But I will not stir
from this place, do what they can: I will walk up   125
and down here, and I will sing, that they shall
hear I am not afraid.
[Sings]
The ousel cock so black of hue,
    With orange-tawny bill,

---

109.   *about a round:* (1) in a dance (2) by a roundabout route.

121.   *translated:* transformed.

128.   *ousel:* blackbird.

The throstle with his note so true,   130
   The wren with little quill.

Titania *[Waking]* What angel wakes me from my flowery bed?

Bottom *[Sings]* The finch, the sparrow, and the lark,
The plain-song cuckoo grey,
Whose note full many a man doth mark,   135
And dares not answer nay—
for, indeed, who would set his wit to so foolish
a bird? Who would give a bird the lie, though
he cry 'cuckoo' never so?

Titania I pray thee, gentle mortal, sing again;   140
Mine ear is much enamoured of thy note.
So is mine eye enthrallèd to thy shape;
And thy fair virtue's force perforce doth move me,
On the first view, to say, to swear, I love thee.

Bottom Methinks, mistress, you should have little reason   145
For that: and yet, to say the truth, reason and
love keep little company together now-a-days:
the more the pity that some honest neighbours
will not make them friends. Nay, I can gleek
upon occasion.   150

Titania Thou art as wise as thou art beautiful.

Bottom Not so, neither; but if I had wit enough to get out of
this wood, I have enough to serve mine own turn.

Titania Out of this wood do not desire to go: 155
Thou shalt remain here, whether thou wilt or no.
I am a spirit of no common rate,
The summer still doth tend upon my state;
And I do love thee: therefore, go with me,
I'll give thee fairies to attend on thee,   160
And they shall fetch thee jewels from the deep,

130. *throstle:* thrush.

131. *little quill:* thin voice.

134. *plain-song:* simple, one-line (church) music.

143. *fair virtue's force:* the power of your beauty and your moral greatness.

perforce: of necessity.

149. *gleek:* make jokes.

157. *rate:* value.

And sing, while thou on pressèd flowers dost sleep;
And I will purge thy mortal grossness so
That thou shalt like an airy spirit go.
Peasblossom, Cobweb, Mote, and Mustardseed!   165
[Enter Four Fairies]

Peaseblossom Ready.

Cobweb And I.

Mote And I.

Mustardseed Where shall we go?

Titania Be kind and courteous to this gentleman:
Hop in his walks and gambol in his eyes;
Feed him with apricocks and dewberries,
With purple grapes, green figs, and mulberries;   170
The honey bags steal from the humble-bees,
And, for night-tapers, crop their waxen thighs,
And light them at the fiery glow-worm's eyes,
To have my love to bed and to arise;
And pluck the wings from painted butterflies   175
To fan the moonbeams from his sleeping eyes:
Nod to him, elves, and do him courtesies.

Peaseblossom Hail, mortal!

Cobweb Hail!

Mote Hail!   180

Mustardseed Hail!

Bottom I cry your worships mercy, heartily. I beseech
Your worship's name.

Cobweb Cobweb.

Bottom I shall desire you of more acquaintance, good   185
Master Cobweb. If I cut my finger, I shall make
bold with you. Your name, honest gentleman?

169. *dewberries:* blackberries.

182. *cry your worships mercy:* beg your pardon, sirs.

186. *make bold with you:* be so bold as to use you (to dress my wound).

Peaseblossom Peaseblossom.

Bottom I pray you, commend me to Mistress Squash,   190
your mother, and to Master Peascod, your
father. Good Master Peaseblossom, I shall desire you of more acquaintance too. Your name,
I beseech you, sir?

Mustardseed Mustardseed.   195

Bottom Good Master Mustardseed, I know your patience well: That same cowardly, giant-like ox-
beef hath devoured many a gentleman of your
house. I promise you, your kindred hath made
my eyes water ere now. I desire you of more ac-   200
quaintance, good Master Mustardseed.

Titania Come, wait upon him. Lead him to my bower.
The moon, methinks, looks with a watery eye,
  And when she weeps, weeps every little flower,
Lamenting some enforcèd chastity.   205
  Tie up my love's tongue, bring him silently.
[Exeunt]

---

190.   *Squash:* unripe peascod.

191.   *Peascod:* pea pod (a folk-remedy for lovesickness).

196.   *patience:* suffering.

199.   *kindred:* relatives.

202.   *bower:* (1) shady retreat (2) (lady's) private room.

COMMENTARY

Titania remains asleep, but the mechanicals do not notice her when they enter. Their speech is written in prose, which contrasts sharply with the complex poetry of the previous scene. Bottom speaks first, before Quince can call the group to order. Even so, Quince addresses Bottom affectionately, calling him "bully Bottom," a term of endearment. Bottom is full of himself, but his companions clearly still like him.

Quince says that they have arrived at an excellent spot for their rehearsal: The patch of green they are standing in will make a wonderful stage, and the hawthorn thicket next to it will serve as

their dressing room. There is comedy in Quince's words, because the "green plot" really is a stage, and the stage property representing the "hawthorn brake" would have been placed in front of the door behind the stage that led to the theatre's real "tiring-house" (changing room). Shakespeare's audiences would have recognized the humor, but they also may have pondered another variation on Shakespeare's theme of the difference between appearance and reality. We know that when we watch *A Midsummer Night's Dream*, we see real men—actors—pretending to be fictional characters, who are actors pretending to be other fictional characters. The real actors are standing on a real stage, which they expect the audience to believe is a wood near Athens many centuries ago. In this rehearsal for the play-within-a-play, the actor playing Quince points to the real stage he is standing on and says, "This green plot shall be our stage." It is as if Shakespeare is holding a mirror up to a mirror and leaving us to wonder which of the many images we see is real.

There is more comedy and further allusion to the theme of appearance versus reality in Bottom's absurd suggestion that in order to avoid frightening the ladies in the audience, the mechanicals should begin their performance by announcing that they are only pretending to be the characters in their play. His belief that anyone would be convinced by his onstage suicide as Pyramus is ridiculous. Part of Shakespeare's joke here is that his audience would have been familiar with the horrific revenge plays (such as Thomas Kyd's *The Spanish Tragedy*) that were popular during his lifetime. Such plays featured onstage mutilation, torture, and killing, and they were genuinely and sensationally shocking. The idea that the "rude mechanicals" could achieve such an effect is ludicrous.

When Quince agrees to write a prologue in "eight and six" (alternating lines of eight and six syllables), Bottom characteristically goes over the top and insists it should be in "eight and eight," as if the higher numbers in themselves would make it better. When Snout and Starveling say they are worried that the ladies might also be frightened by the appearance of a lion in their play, Bottom decides that Snug must wear a mask that reveals half of his real face, and that he must announce (with exaggerated courtesy) that he is really only an actor.

Just as silly is Bottom's suggestion that the effect of moonshine can be achieved by leaving the window open to let the real moon shine in, without any thought as to whether the sky might be cloudy or not. Quince's idea that a man with a lantern should represent the moon is more practical, but the language in which he suggests it shows his stupidity: He uses the malapropism "disfigure" when he should say "figure" or "represent." Bottom decides that they must have an actor represent the wall that separates Pyramus and Thisbe, and the crack through which they speak should be represented by a gap made between the actor's fingers. It is clear to the audience that this attempt at high drama is going to fall comically flat. When Puck appears, he accurately refers to the mechanicals as "hempen homespuns" that are "swaggering"—that is, simple folk who have ideas far above their abilities.

The comedy continues as the mechanicals begin their rehearsal. Bottom gets his first line wrong and then exits. Flute's speech, as Thisbe, is absurdly puffed-up. Flute ends by likening Pyramus to a horse, at which point Bottom returns, his head having been turned into the head of an ass. His companions flee in terror at the sight, and Puck mischievously tells the audience that he will lead them on a wild goose chase through the wood.

Bottom does not realize what has happened to him, and when Snout and Quince briefly return and tell him he has been changed, he thinks they are playing a joke on him. Believing himself to be alone, he sings to himself to keep up his spirits. His singing wakes Titania, who sees him and instantly falls in love with him. His voice would necessarily be ridiculous and unmusical, for he has the head, mouth, and tongue of an ass. Titania, though, is smitten by his music, which the audience would recognize as very unlike the beautiful lullaby that earlier sent her to sleep. She begs him to sing again and declares her love for him. Bottom readily accepts that she loves him, even though it is apparently unreasonable, for "to say the truth, reason and love keep little company together now-a-days."

Bottom and Titania.
Clive Barda/PAL

The absurd mismatch between Bottom and Titania is seen not only in their very different appearances, but also in their speech. Bottom speaks in down-to-earth prose, in a conversational style, while Titania speaks in elevated verse, in rhyming couplets. When she says to him "Thou art as wise as thou art beautiful," she unknowingly speaks the truth: Bottom is foolish and ugly in equal measure. In her eyes, though, he is beauty itself, and she promises him a life with her in which he will be spoiled by the attentions of her fairies. She calls four of them to serve him directly. Their names—Peaseblossom, Cobweb, Mote (or Moth), and Mustardseed—define them as tiny and delicate. (A *mote* is a tiny speck of dust, while a moth is a small winged insect. In Shakespeare's time, the fairy's name would have been pronounced as "Mote," and Shakespeare probably intended the name to carry both ideas.)

Titania instructs the four fairies to look after Bottom in a speech that is rich with sensuous and beautiful imagery and focuses the imagination on the exquisite detail of the tiniest of creatures. The fairies instantly hail him, and they tell him their names in turn. He tells them he is keen to get to know them, and Titania orders them to lead him to her bower. She notices that the moon looks watery, which she takes as a sign that sexual fulfillment is being frustrated in the world. Her comment reminds the audience of the several broken relationships in the play that have yet to be healed. The scene closes on a farcical note with her request that Bottom's tongue should be tied up, which suggests that he is making braying noises that he cannot control.

Act III, Scene 2

Another part of the wood. Oberon realizes that Puck has put a spell on Lysander by mistake, so he himself puts some of the juice in Demetrius' eyes to make him fall in love with Helena. Demetrius and Lysander quarrel over her. Oberon resolves to put everything right through magic.

ACT III, SCENE 2

[Enter OBERON, King of the Fairies]

Oberon I wonder if Titania be awaked;
Then, what it was that next came in her eye,
Which she must dote on in extremity.
[Enter PUCK]
Here comes my messenger. How now, mad spirit?
What night-rule now about this haunted grove?   5

Puck My mistress with a monster is in love.
Near to her close and consecrated bower,
While she was in her dull and sleeping hour,
A crew of patches, rude mechanicals,
That work for bread upon Athenian stalls,   10
Were met together to rehearse a play
Intended for great Theseus' nuptial day.
The shallowest thickskin of that barren sort
Who Pyramus presented in their sport,
Forsook his scene and entered in a brake,   15
When I did him at this advantage take:
An ass's nole I fixèd on his head.
Anon, his Thisbe must be answered,
And forth my mimic comes. When they him spy—
As wild geese that the creeping fowler eye,   20
Or russet-pated choughs, many in sort,
Rising and cawing at the gun's report,
Sever themselves and madly sweep the sky—
So at his sight away his fellows fly,
And at our stamp here, o'er and o'er one falls;   25
He 'Murder!' cries, and help from Athens calls.
Their sense thus weak, lost with their fears, thus strong,

NOTES

5.   *night-rule:* disorders of the night.

9.   *patches:* fools.

      rude mechanicals: rough working-men.

13.   *barren sort:* dull-witted group.

17.   *nole:* head.

18.   *Anon:* immediately.

19.   *mimic:* actor.

21.   *russet-pated choughs, many in sort:* large flock of jackdaws (birds) with dull-colored heads.

23.   *Sever themselves:* scatter.

25.   *at our stamp:* when we (I) stamp.

Made senseless things begin to do them wrong,
For briars and thorns at their apparel snatch,
Some sleeves, some hats; from yielders all things catch.   30
I led them on in this distracted fear,
And left sweet Pyramus translated there;
When in that moment, so it came to pass,
Titania waked, and straightway loved an ass.

Oberon This falls out better than I could devise.   35
But hast thou yet latched the Athenian's eyes
With the love juice, as I did bid thee do?

Puck I took him sleeping—that is finished too—
And the Athenian woman by his side,
That, when he waked, of force she must be eyed.   40
[*Enter DEMETRIUS and HERMIA*]

Oberon Stand close; this is the same Athenian.

Puck This is the woman, but not this the man.

Demetrius O, why rebuke you him that loves you so?
Lay breath so bitter on your bitter foe.

Hermia Now I but chide, but I should use thee worse,   45
For thou, I fear, hast given me cause to curse.
If thou hast slain Lysander in his sleep,
Being o'er shoes in blood, plunge in the deep,
And kill me too.
The sun was not so true unto the day   50
As he to me: would he have stol'n away
From sleeping Hermia? I'll believe as soon
This whole earth may be bored, and that the moon
May through the centre creep and so displease
Her brother's noontide with th' Antipodes.   55
It cannot be but thou hast murdered him.
So should a murderer look: so dead, so grim.

30. *from yielders all things catch:* everything catches at those who give in (to fear).

32. *translated:* transformed.

36. *latched:* caught.

41. *close:* i.e., where you will not be seen.

45. *chide:* scold.

48. *Being o'er shoes in blood:* i.e., having waded in so far.

53. *This whole earth may be bored:* that a hole could be drilled through this solid earth.

57. *dead:* deadly.

Demetrius So should the murdered look, and so should I,
Pierced through the heart with your stern cruelty;
Yet you, the murderer, look as bright, as clear,   60
As yonder Venus in her glimmering sphere.

Hermia What's this to my Lysander? Where is he?
Ah, good Demetrius, wilt thou give him me?

Demetrius I had rather give his carcass to my hounds.

Hermia Out, dog! Out, cur! Thou driv'st me past the bounds   65
Of maiden's patience. Hast thou slain him, then?
Henceforth be never numbered among men!
Oh. Once tell true; tell true, even for my sake:
Durst thou have looked upon him being awake?
And hast thou killed him sleeping? O brave touch!   70
Could not a worm, an adder, do so much?
An adder did it; for with doubler tongue
Than thine, thou serpent, never adder stung.

Demetrius You spend your passion on a misprised mood:
I am not guilty of Lysander's blood,   75
Nor is he dead, for aught that I can tell.

Hermia I pray thee, tell me, then, that he is well.

Demetrius And if I could, what should I get therefor?

Hermia A privilege never to see me more.
And from thy hated presence part I so.   80
See me no more, whether he be dead or no.
[Exit]

Demetrius There is no following her in this fierce vein;
Here, therefore, for a while I will remain.
So sorrow's heaviness doth heavier grow
For debt that bankrupt sleep doth sorrow owe;   85

61.   *Venus:* (1) evening star (2) goddess of love.

sphere: orbit.

70.   *O brave touch!:* A courageous stroke! (sarcastic).

74.   *misprised:* mistaken.

76.   *for aught that I can tell:* for all I know.

78.   *therefor:* for it, in return.

83.   *in this fierce vein:* when she is angry like this.

Which now in some slight measure it will pay,
If for his tender here I make some stay.
[Lies down]

Oberon What hast thou done? Thou hast mistaken quite,
And laid the love-juice on some true-love's sight:
Of thy misprision must perforce ensue   90
Some true love turned, and not a false turned true.

Puck Then fate o'er-rules, that, one man holding troth,
A million fail, confounding oath on oath.

Oberon About the wood go, swifter than the wind,
And Helena of Athens look thou find.   95
All fancy-sick she is, and pale of cheer,
With sighs of love, that costs the fresh blood dear.
By some illusion see thou bring her here;
I'll charm his eyes against she do appear.

Puck I go, I go; look how I go,   100
Swifter than arrow from the Tartar's bow!
[Exit]

Oberon Flower of this purple dye,
Hit with Cupid's archery,
Sink in apple of his eye!
[He drops the juice on DEMETRIUS' eyelids]
When his love he doth espy,   105
Let her shine as gloriously
As the Venus of the sky.
When thou wak'st, if she be by,
Beg of her for remedy.
[Enter PUCK]

Puck Captain of our fairy band,   110
Helena is here at hand,
And the youth mistook by me,
Pleading for a lover's fee.

90. *misprision:* mistake.

92–93. *Then fate . . . oath:* In that case, fate is in charge, because for every man that is true in love, a million fail, repeatedly breaking their word.

96. *fancy-sick:* love-sick.

cheer: face.

97. *costs the fresh blood dear:* (Sighing was thought to use up blood.)

99. *against:* in preparation for the time when.

101. *Tartar's bow:* Turk's bow (thought to be very powerful).

104. *apple:* pupil.

113. *fee:* reward.

Shall we their fond pageant see?
Lord, what fools these mortals be!   115

Oberon Stand aside. The noise they make
Will cause Demetrius to awake.

Puck Then will two at once woo one.
That must needs be sport alone;
And those things do best please me
That befall prepost'rously.   120
[Enter LYSANDER and HELENA]

Lysander Why should you think that I should woo in scorn?
Scorn and derision never come in tears.
    Look when I vow, I weep; and vows so born,
In their nativity all truth appears.   125
    How can these things in me seem scorn to you,
        Bearing the badge of faith to prove them true?

Helena You do advance your cunning more and more.
When truth kills truth, O devilish-holy fray!
These vows are Hermia's. Will you give her o'er?   130
Weigh oath with oath, and you will nothing weigh:
Your vows to her and me, put in two scales,
Will even weigh, and both as light as tales.

Lysander I had no judgment when to her I swore.

Helena Nor none, in my mind, now you give her o'er.   135

Lysander Demetrius loves her, and he loves not you.

Demetrius *[Waking]* O Helen, goddess, nymph, perfect, divine!
To what, my love, shall I compare thine eyne?
Crystal is muddy. O, how ripe in show
Thy lips, those kissing cherries, tempting grow!   140
That pure congealèd white, high Taurus' snow,

114. *fond pageant:* foolish spectacle.

118. *alone:* by itself.

123. *Look when:* whenever.

vows so born: vows that are born (in tears).

125. *In their nativity all truth appears:* Nothing but truth appears at their birth.

127. *badge of faith:* i.e., his tears.

133. *tales:* false stories.

137. *nymph:* beautiful and divine woodland creature.

138. *eyne:* eyes.

141. *Taurus':* a mountain range in Turkey.

Fanned with the eastern wind, turns to a crow
When thou hold'st up thy hand. O, let me kiss
This princess of pure white, this seal of bliss!

Helena O spite! O hell! I see you all are bent   145
To set against me for your merriment.
If you were civil, and knew courtesy,
You would not do me thus much injury.
Can you not hate me, as I know you do,
But you must join in souls to mock me too?   150
If you were men, as men you are in show,
You would not use a gentle lady so,
To vow, and swear, and superpraise my parts,
When I am sure you hate me with your hearts.
You both are rivals, and love Hermia;   155
And now both rivals, to mock Helena.
A trim exploit, a manly enterprise,
To conjure tears up in a poor maid's eyes
With your derision! None of noble sort
Would so offend a virgin, and extort   160
A poor soul's patience, all to make you sport.

Lysander You are unkind, Demetrius. Be not so.
For you love Hermia: this you know I know.
And here, with all good will, with all my heart,
In Hermia's love I yield you up my part;   165
And yours of Helena to me bequeath,
Whom I do love and will do till my death.

Helena Never did mockers waste more idle breath.

Demetrius Lysander, keep thy Hermia; I will none.
If e'er I loved her, all that love is gone.   170
My heart to her but as guest-wise sojourned;
And now to Helen is it home returned,
There to remain.

Lysander Helen, it is not so.

144.   *seal:* the suggestion is of taking the hand in marriage.

160–161.   *extort:* force such suffering from a poor soul.

166.   *bequeath:* assign.

169.   *I will none:* I want no part of her.

171.   *sojourned:* stayed with on a visit.

Demetrius Disparage not the faith thou dost not know,
Lest, to thy peril, thou aby it dear.   175
Look where thy love comes: yonder is thy dear.
[Enter HERMIA]

Hermia Dark night, that from the eye his function takes,
The ear more quick of apprehension makes;
Wherein it doth impair the seeing sense,
It pays the hearing double recompense: 180
Thou art not by mine eye, Lysander, found;
Mine ear, I thank it, brought me to thy sound.
But why unkindly didst thou leave me so?

Lysander Why should he stay whom love doth press to go?

Hermia What love could press Lysander from my side?   185

Lysander Lysander's love, that would not let him bide:
Fair Helena, who more engilds the night
Than all yon fiery oes and eyes of light.
Why seek'st thou me? Could not this make thee know
The hate I bare thee made me leave thee so?   190

Hermia You speak not as you think; it cannot be.

Helena Lo, she is one of this confederacy!
Now I perceive they have conjoined all three
To fashion this false sport in spite of me.
Injurious Hermia! Most ungrateful maid,   195
Have you conspired, have you with these contrived,
To bait me with this foul derision?
Is all the counsel that we two have shared,
The sisters' vows, the hours that we have spent,
When we have chid the hasty-footed time   200
For parting us,—O, is all forgot?
All schooldays' friendship, childhood innocence?
We, Hermia, like two artificial gods,
Have with our needles created both one flower,

---

175. *aby:* buy.

188. *oes and eyes of light:* i.e., stars. "Oes" were spangles that decorated dresses. (Note the pun on the letters of the alphabet.)

203. *artificial:* highly skilled in art.

204. *needles:* pronounced "neelds."

Both on one sampler, sitting on one cushion,   205
Both warbling of one song, both in one key;
As if our hands, our sides, voices, and minds
Had been incorporate. So we grew together,
Like to a double cherry, seeming parted;
But yet an union in partition,   210
Two lovely berries moulded on one stem;
So, with two seeming bodies, but one heart;
Two of the first, like coats in heraldry,
Due but to one, and crownèd with one crest.
And will you rent our ancient love asunder,   215
To join with men in scorning your poor friend?
It is not friendly, 'tis not maidenly:
Our sex, as well as I, may chide you for it,
Though I alone do feel the injury.

Hermia I am amazèd at your passionate words: 220
I scorn you not; it seems that you scorn me.

Helena Have you not set Lysander, as in scorn,
To follow me, and praise my eyes and face?
And made your other love, Demetrius,
Who even but now did spurn me with his foot,   225
To call me goddess, nymph, divine, and rare,
Precious, celestial? Wherefore speaks he this
To her he hates? And wherefore doth Lysander
Deny your love, so rich within his soul,
And tender me, forsooth, affection,   230
But by your setting on, by your consent?
What though I be not so in grace as you,
So hung upon with love, so fortunate,
But miserable most, to love unloved:
This you should pity rather than despise.   235

Hermia I understand not what you mean by this.

Helena Ay, do! Persever, counterfeit sad looks,

---

205. *sampler:* piece of embroidery done to demonstrate skill.

208. *incorporate:* of one body.

213. *coats in heraldry:* coats of arms.

214. *crownèd with one crest:* topped by one heraldic crest (an image that appears above the shield).

227. *Wherefore:* why.

230. *forsooth:* in truth.

237. *Persever:* stressed on the second syllable.

Make mouths upon me when I turn my back,
Wink each at other; hold the sweet jest up.
This sport, well carried, shall be chronicled.   240
If you have any pity, grace, or manners,
You would not make me such an argument.
But fare ye well: 'tis partly my own fault;
Which death, or absence, soon shall remedy.

Lysander Stay, gentle Helena; hear my excuse;   245
My love, my life, my soul, fair Helena!

Helena O excellent!

Hermia *[to LYSANDER]* Sweet, do not scorn her so.

Demetrius *[to LYSANDER]* If she cannot entreat, I can compel.

Lysander Thou canst compel no more than she entreat;
Thy threats have no more strength than her weak prayers.   250
Helen, I love thee; by my life I do.
I swear by that which I will lose for thee
To prove him false that says I love thee not.

Demetrius *[to HELENA]* I say I love thee more than he can do.

Lysander If thou say so, withdraw, and prove it too.   255

Demetrius Quick, come–

Hermia Lysander, whereto tends all this?

Lysander Away, you Ethiop!

Demetrius No, no, sir,
Seem to break loose; take on as you would follow,
But yet come not. You are a tame man, go.

Lysander Hang off, thou cat, thou burr! Vile thing, let loose,   260
Or I will shake thee from me like a serpent.

Hermia Why are you grown so rude? What change is this,
Sweet love?

Lysander Thy love! Out, tawny Tartar, out!
Out, loathèd medicine! O hated potion, hence!

238. *make mouths upon:* mock.

242. *argument:* topic, object.

255. *withdraw:* draw your sword.

257. *Ethiop:* black person,

260. *burr:* (burrs are hard to shake off),

263. *Tartar:* Turk.

Hermia Do you not jest?

Helena Yes, sooth; and so do you.   265

Lysander Demetrius, I will keep my word with thee.

Demetrius I would I had your bond; for I perceive
   A weak bond holds you; I'll not trust your word.

Lysander What! Should I hurt her, strike her, kill her dead?
   Although I hate her, I'll not harm her so.   270

Hermia What! Can you do me greater harm than hate?
   Hate me? Wherefore? O me! What news, my love?
   Am not I Hermia? Are not you Lysander?
   I am as fair now as I was erewhile.
   Since night you loved me; yet since night you left me: 275
   Why then, you left me—O, the gods forbid!—
   In earnest, shall I say?

Lysander Ay, by my life;
   And never did desire to see thee more.
   Therefore be out of hope, of question, doubt,
   Be certain, nothing truer; 'tis no jest   280
   That I do hate thee and love Helena.

Hermia *[to HELENA]* O me! You juggler! You cankerblossom!
   You thief of love! What, have you come by night,
   And stol'n my love's heart from him?

Helena Fine, i' faith!
   Have you no modesty, no maiden shame,   285
   No touch of bashfulness? What, will you tear
   Impatient answers from my gentle tongue?
   Fie, fie! you counterfeit, you puppet, you!

Hermia 'Puppet'? Why so? Ay, that way goes the game.
   Now I perceive that she hath made compare   290

282.   *juggler:* trickster.

282.   *cankerblossom:* canker-worm, a grub
that destroys flowers.

288.   *counterfeit:* cheat.

Between our statures; she hath urged her height;
And with her personage, her tall personage,
Her height, forsooth, she hath prevailed with him.
And are you grown so high in his esteem
Because I am so dwarfish and so low?   295
How low am I, thou painted maypole? Speak!
How low am I? I am not yet so low
But that my nails can reach unto thine eyes.

Helena I pray you, though you mock me, gentlemen,
Let her not hurt me. I was never curst;   300
I have no gift at all in shrewishness.
I am a right maid for my cowardice;
Let her not strike me. You perhaps may think,
Because she is something lower than myself,
That I can match her.

Hermia Lower? Hark, again.   305

Helena Good Hermia, do not be so bitter with me.
I evermore did love you, Hermia,
Did ever keep your counsels, never wronged you;
Save that in love unto Demetrius
I told him of your stealth unto this wood.   310
He followed you; for love I followed him;
But he hath chid me hence, and threatened me
To strike me, spurn me, nay, to kill me too.
And now, so you will let me quiet go,
To Athens will I bear my folly back,   315
And follow you no farther. Let me go.
You see how simple and how fond I am.

Hermia Why, get you gone! Who is't that hinders you?

Helena A foolish heart that I leave here behind.

Hermia What! with Lysander?

Helena With Demetrius.   320

296.   *maypole:* tall and thin person.

Lysander Be not afraid; she shall not harm thee, Helena.

Demetrius No, sir, she shall not, though you take her part.

Helena O, when she's angry, she is keen and shrewd:
She was a vixen when she went to school;
And, though she be but little, she is fierce.   325

Hermia 'Little' again! Nothing but 'low' and 'little'!
Why will you suffer her to flout me thus?
Let me come to her.

Lysander Get you gone, you dwarf,
You minimus of hind'ring knot-grass made,
You bead, you acorn.

Demetrius You are too officious   330
In her behalf that scorns your services.
Let her alone: speak not of Helena,
Take not her part; for if thou dost intend
Never so little show of love to her,
Thou shalt aby it.

Lysander Now she holds me not;   335
Now follow, if thou dar'st, to try whose right,
Of thine or mine, is most in Helena.

Demetrius Follow? Nay, I'll go with thee, cheek by jowl.
[Exeunt LYSANDER and DEMETRIUS]

Hermia You, mistress, all this coil is 'long of you:
Nay, go not back.

Helena I will not trust you, I;   340
Nor longer stay in your curst company.
Your hands than mine are quicker for a fray;
My legs are longer though, to run away.
[Exit]

Hermia I am amazed, and know not what to say.

---

324. *vixen:* female fox.

329. *minimus:* tiny, insignificant creature.

knot-grass: creeping weed, which in folk medicine was believed to stunt growth.

338. *cheek by jowl:* immediately beside you.

339. *all this coil is 'long of you:* all this trouble is down to you.

342. *quicker for a fray:* quicker to get involved in a fight.

356. *welkin:* sky.

[Exit]
[OBERON and PUCK come forward]

Oberon This is thy negligence: still thou mistak'st,   345
  Or else commit'st thy knaveries wilfully.

Puck Believe me, King of Shadows, I mistook.
  Did not you tell me I should know the man
  By the Athenian garments he had on?
  And so far blameless proves my enterprise   350
  That I have 'nointed an Athenian's eyes:
  And so far am I glad it so did sort,
  As this their jangling I esteem a sport.

Oberon Thou seest these lovers seek a place to fight:
  Hie therefore, Robin, overcast the night;   355
  The starry welkin cover thou anon
  With drooping fog as black as Acheron,
  And lead these testy rivals so astray
  As one come not within another's way.
  Like to Lysander sometime frame thy tongue,   360
  Then stir Demetrius up with bitter wrong,
  And sometime rail thou like Demetrius;
  And from each other look thou lead them thus,
  Till o'er their brows death-counterfeiting sleep
  With leaden legs and batty wings doth creep.   365
  Then crush this herb into Lysander's eye;
  Whose liquor hath this virtuous property,
  To take from thence all error with his might
  And make his eyeballs roll with wonted sight.
  When they next wake, all this derision   370
  Shall seem a dream and fruitless vision,
  And back to Athens shall the lovers wend
  With league whose date till death shall never end.
  Whiles I in this affair do thee employ,
  I'll to my queen, and beg her Indian boy;   375
  And then I will her charmèd eye release
  From monster's view, and all things shall be peace.

357. *Acheron:* one of the four rivers of the underworld.

359. *As:* so that.

365. *batty:* bat-like.

368. *his:* its.

369. *wonted:* accustomed.

Puck My fairy lord, this must be done with haste,
For night's swift dragons cut the clouds full fast,
And yonder shines Aurora's harbinger,   380
At whose approach ghosts, wandering here and there,
Troop home to churchyards. Damnèd spirits all,
That in cross-ways and floods have burial,
Already to their wormy beds are gone,
For fear lest day should look their shames upon.   385
They wilfully exile themselves from light,
And must for aye consort with black-browed night.

Oberon But we are spirits of another sort.
I with the morning's love have oft made sport;
And like a forester the groves may tread   390
Even till the eastern gate, all fiery-red,
Opening on Neptune with fair blessèd beams,
Turns into yellow gold his salt-green streams.
But, notwithstanding, haste, make no delay:
We may effect this business yet ere day.   395
[Exit]

Puck Up and down, up and down;
I will lead them up and down:
I am feared in field and town.
Goblin, lead them up and down.
Here comes one.   400
[Enter LYSANDER]

Lysander Where art thou, proud Demetrius? Speak thou now.

Puck Here, villain, drawn and ready. Where art thou?

Lysander I will be with thee straight.

Puck Follow me, then,
To plainer ground.
[Exit LYSANDER]
[Enter DEMETRIUS]

380. *Aurora's harbinger:* the morning star, herald of the dawn.

382. *Damnèd spirits:* the ghosts of the damned. People who committed suicide were believed to be damned and were buried not in consecrated ground, but at crossroads.

387. *aye:* ever.

389. *I with the morning's love have oft made sport:* (1) I have made love with Aurora in the morning. (2) I have gone hunting in the morning (with Aurora's lover).

390. *forester:* forest gamekeeper.

392. *Neptune:* god of the sea.

402. *drawn:* with your sword drawn.

403. *straight:* immediately.

plainer: more open.

Demetrius Lysander! speak again.
Thou runaway, thou coward, art thou fled?   405
Speak! In some bush? Where dost thou hide thy head?

Puck Thou coward, art thou bragging to the stars,
Telling the bushes that thou look'st for wars,
And wilt not come? Come, recreant, come, thou child,
I'll whip thee with a rod: he is defiled   410
That draws a sword on thee.

409.   *recreant:* coward.

410.   *defiled:* tainted, degraded.

Demetrius Yea, art thou there?

Puck Follow my voice; we'll try no manhood here.
[Exeunt]
[Enter LYSANDER]

412.   *try no manhood:* not put manhood to the test.

Lysander He goes before me, and still dares me on;
When I come where he calls, then he is gone.
The villain is much lighter heeled than I;   415
I followed fast, but faster he did fly;
That fallen am I in dark uneven way,
And here will rest me. Come, thou gentle day!
[Lies down]
For if but once thou show me thy grey light,
I'll find Demetrius, and revenge this spite.   420
[Sleeps]
[Enter PUCK and DEMETRIUS]

Puck Ho, ho, ho! Coward, why com'st thou not?

Demetrius Abide me, if thou dar'st; for well I wot
Thou runn'st before me, shifting every place,
And dar'st not stand, nor look me in the face.
Where art thou now?

422.   *Abide:* face, encounter.

        wot: know.

Puck Come hither; I am here.   425

Demetrius Nay, then, thou mock'st me. Thou shalt buy this dear,
If ever I thy face by daylight see.
Now, go thy way. Faintness constraineth me

428.   *constraineth:* forces.

To measure out my length on this cold bed.
By day's approach look to be visited. 430
[Sleeps]
[Enter HELENA]

Helena O weary night, O long and tedious night,
Abate thy hours; shine comforts from the east,
That I may back to Athens by daylight,
From these that my poor company detest;
And sleep, that sometimes shuts up sorrow's eye, 435
Steal me awhile from mine own company.
[Sleeps]

Puck Yet but three? Come one more;
Two of both kinds makes up four.
Here she comes, curst and sad:
Cupid is a knavish lad, 440
Thus to make poor females mad.
[Enter HERMIA]

Hermia Never so weary, never so in woe,
Bedabbled with the dew, and torn with briers,
I can no further crawl, no further go.
My legs can keep no pace with my desires. 445
Here will I rest me till the break of day.
Heavens shield Lysander, if they mean a fray!
[Sleeps]

Puck On the ground
Sleep sound.
I'll apply 450
To your eye,
Gentle lover, remedy.
[Squeezes the juice on LYSANDER'S eyes]
When thou wak'st,
Thou tak'st
True delight 455
In the sight
Of thy former lady's eye:

432. *Abate:* shorten.

And the country proverb known,
That every man should take his own,
In your waking shall be shown: 460
Jack shall have Jill;
Nought shall go ill;
The man shall have his mare again, and all shall be well.
[Exit PUCK]

461.   *Jack shall . . . all shall be well:* (a series of proverbs).

COMMENTARY

Oberon wonders whether Titania has woken up yet, and if so, what creature she has first seen and fallen in love with. Puck arrives to tell him the news: "My mistress with a monster is in love." He describes what has happened in the previous scene, which is news to Oberon but not to the audience. Shakespeare's purpose here is to extract even more humor from the events by retelling them as seen through the eyes of Puck. His dramatic and expressive imagery adds another level of comedy, just as in real life we relate comic tales colorfully to people who already know what has happened but enjoy being reminded how funny the story was the first time. This summary of what has happened earlier is also useful in getting performances of the play going again if there has been an intermission, which is usually placed after Act III, Scene 1.

Puck's description is mercilessly detailed. In rhyming couplets, he describes Bottom and his companions as "A crew of patches, rude mechanicals." A "patch" is a clown, jester, or fool—a person who is funny on purpose. These rough workmen think they are highly serious but in reality are absurdly amusing. The worst of them is Bottom, whom Puck calls "The shallowest thick skin of that barren sort." His description of how Bottom's companions react to his return with the ass's head is particularly vivid: They scatter like a flock of birds at the sound of a gun. His language

cleverly captures the sense of panic: The birds "[s]ever themselves and madly sweep the sky," an image that creates a picture of the mechanicals flapping their arms about and not knowing which way to go in their confusion. Puck's reference to a gun is an *anachronism* (a use of a term that could not have been known at the time), but it is not a mistake. The "rude mechanicals" are characters drawn from the England of Shakespeare's own time; they are Athenian in name only. Shakespeare does not intend to re-create Athens or the nearby wood in any detail, or to fix the events of the play in any particular time.

Puck tells Oberon that he has also "latch'd the Athenian's eyes / With the love juice," but when Demetrius and Hermia enter, it becomes clear that Puck has applied the magic to the wrong person. Demetrius is trying to persuade Hermia to love him, but she angrily rejects him. She fears that he has murdered Lysander as he slept. She cannot believe Lysander would have left her voluntarily, for "[t]he sun was not so true unto the day / As he to me." Demetrius picks up the word "murderer" from Hermia's speech and plays with it: He says that if anyone is a murderer, it is Hermia, because she is killing him with her "stern cruelty." Hermia describes her love for Lysander in terms of the "sun," the "moon," and the "earth"—cosmic images that convey intensity. Demetrius replies in a similar vein, likening her beauty to that of Venus, the evening star and goddess of love. Demetrius tells her that for all he knows, Lysander is alive, and he certainly hasn't killed him. Hermia storms off to avoid his "hated presence." Exhausted by all the excitement, Demetrius lies down and falls asleep.

Oberon tells Puck to correct his mistake by finding Helena and leading her back to Demetrius, whose eyes he will meanwhile charm so that when he wakes up and sees Helena he will fall in love with her and all will be well. In the time that it takes Oberon to administer the magic juice, Puck has returned with Helena and Lysander, exclaiming "Lord, what fools these mortals be!" It is a doubly comic observation: People can certainly behave foolishly when they are in love, but in this case at least some of that foolishness has been caused by Puck's own mistake. (It is, however, a comment that can be applied fairly to the absurd pretensions of the "rude mechanicals" that Puck has described a little earlier.) Puck reminds us that he is happies when things turn out ridiculously: "And those things do best please me / That befall preposterously."

Lysander asks Helena how she can think he is mocking her by protesting his love. He is wearing the badge of faith, his tears. She replies that he has previously expressed the "truth" of his love to Hermia with equal intensity; his promises to each of them are of equally little value. Lysander says that Demetrius does not love her, but at that instant Demetrius wakes, sees Helena, and falls instantly in love with her. The rhyme scheme breaks for a line, interrupting the rhythm to make his waking more dramatic. He describes Helena in a torrent of superlatives: "O Helen, goddess, nymph, perfect, divine!" Significantly, the first physical feature of hers that he refers to is her eyes: "Crystal is muddy" in comparison to them. Just as

extravagant is his comparison of the whiteness of her hands to that of snow, which seems as black as a crow in comparison. Such opposites are frequently found together in *A Midsummer Night's Dream*; they are part of a pattern of imagery that reminds the audience that young love is an extreme, all-or-nothing emotion.

Helena's reply is equally extreme: "O spite! O hell!" She is immediately certain that Demetrius is mocking her. He and Lysander "both are rivals, and love Hermia; / And now both rivals, to mock Helena." As far as she is concerned, "Never did mockers waste more idle breath."

Hermia appears, having found her way to Lysander by hearing his voice. She asks him why he abandoned her and is shocked to hear that he now claims to feel "hate" for her and love for Helena. Hermia can't believe it; Helena believes that Hermia is part of a conspiracy to mock her. She is angry with Hermia, particularly because the two women had previously been so close to each other. Helena describes their friendship as children in a series of images of unity. They had both sat on the same cushion, singing one song, embroidering the same flower on the same sampler. They had grown up together like a double cherry, "Two lovely berries moulded on one stem."

Hermia is "amazèd" by Helena's outrage, replying "I scorn you not; it seems that you scorn me." She cannot understand what is going on. The pattern of long speeches is interrupted by short exchanges as the four lovers argue and insult each other. The words "love" and "hate" are used frequently: life is an all-or-nothing business for these young lovers. Hermia and Helena have a verbal catfight. Hermia calls Helena a "juggler" (that is, a trickster) and a "canker blossom" (a parasite that destroys flowers). Helena calls Hermia a "puppet," which she takes to be a reference to her small-ness. Hermia returns the insult by calling Helena a "painted maypole"—that is, tall and skinny, with too much makeup.

Hermia's rage increases to the point where she threatens to attack Helena physically: "I am not yet so low / But that my nails can reach unto thine eyes." Helena calls upon the men to intervene: "Let her not strike me." Lysander joins in Helena's insults to Hermia's size, using language which is even more scornful and extreme, calling her a "dwarf," a "minimus," a "bead," and an "acorn." Demetrius rebukes him for defending Helena so enthusiastically when she scorns him. The two men storm off to settle the matter once and for all in a fight. Hermia says that all this turmoil is Helena's fault; Helena runs away from her. Hermia once more says that she is "amazed" and then leaves. The effect of all this conflict is comic: The audience knows how the confusion has arisen and that it can be put right by magic.

Oberon and Puck come forward, and Oberon tells Puck that all this chaos is his fault, whether it be by accident or on purpose. Puck defends him-self: Oberon told him to anoint the eyes of a man in Athenian dress, and that is what he did. But he is glad at the way things have turned out, because he enjoys watching the lovers' confused quarrelling. Oberon orders him to create a fog in which Demetrius and Lysander will become separated and thus unable to fight. Puck is to lead them apart by imitating their voices calling to each other. When they finally fall asleep, exhausted, he is to administer an antidote to Lysander. When they

wake, "all this derision / Shall seem a dream and fruitless vision," and then the mortals can return to Athens happily matched forever. The words "dream" and "vision" are important. The first word reminds the audience that they are sharing a dream-like experience; the second is one of the countless references in *A Midsummer Night's Dream* to sight, through which love is perceived. Oberon says that he will go to Titania and ask for "her Indian boy." When she gives him up, Oberon will release her from the spell that has made her fall in love with Bottom, "and all things shall be peace."

Puck urges haste because dawn is fast approaching, when evil spirits return to their graves. But Oberon reminds him (and the audi-ence) that he and Puck are "spirits of another sort." Even so, he orders Puck to be quick so that things can be put right before daybreak. The har-monious ending of the play is in sight. First, though, we witness more comic confusion, as Puck leads Demetrius and Lysander apart, enthusiastically insulting each of them as he pretends to be the other. Exhausted by all this chasing about, Lysander and Demetrius fall asleep. Helena appears, making her way back to Athens. Not see-ing Lysander and Demetrius, she also lies down to sleep. Then Hermia appears and does the same. Puck squeezes the magic juice into Lysander's eyes, accompanied by words spoken in short lines that emphasize the magic of the moment. The deed done, his verse opens out into longer lines, and he closes the scene by announcing that when they all wake up, "all shall be well."

NOTES

NOTES

NOTES

NOTES

NOTES

CLIFFSCOMPLETE

A MIDSUMMER NIGHT'S DREAM
ACT IV

Titania *My Oberon! what visions have I seen!*
Methought I was enamoured of an ass.

Act IV, Scene 1

The Wood. Oberon releases Titania from her spell and they are reconciled. The Duke finds the four lovers in the wood, sees that they are now happily matched, and overrules Egeus. He invites the two couples to be married at his own wedding ceremony.

ACT IV, SCENE 1

[Enter TITANIA, Queen of the Fairies, and BOTTOM, PEASE-BLOSSOM, COBWEB, MOTE, MUSTARDSEED, and other FAIRIES attending; OBERON behind, unseen]

Titania Come, sit thee down upon this flowery bed,
While I thy amiable cheeks do coy,
And stick musk-roses in thy sleek smooth head,
And kiss thy fair large ears, my gentle joy.

Bottom Where's Peaseblossom?   5

Peaseblossom Ready.

Bottom Scratch my head, Peaseblossom.
Where's Monsieur Cobweb?

Cobweb Ready.

Bottom Monsieur Cobweb; good monsieur, get you your   10
weapons in your hand and kill me a red-hipped
humble-bee on the top of a thistle; and, good
monsieur, bring me the honey-bag. Do not fret
yourself too much in the action, monsieur; and,
good monsieur, have a care the honey-bag break   15
not; I would be loath to have you overflown
with a honey-bag, signior. Where's Monsieur
Mustardseed?

Mustardseed Ready.

Bottom Give me your neaf, Monsieur Mustardseed.   20
Pray you, leave your curtesy, good monsieur.

NOTES

2.   *coy:* caress.

8.   *Monsieur:* Bottom addresses the fairies as if they were French (and later, Italian) gentlemen.

20.   *neaf:* fist.

21.   *leave your curtesy:* do please stop bowing.

Mustardseed What's your will?

Bottom Nothing, good monsieur, but to help Cavalery
　　Cobweb to scratch. I must to the barber's, mon-
　　sieur; for methinks I am marvellous hairy about　　　　25
　　the face; and I am such a tender ass, if my hair
　　do but tickle me I must scratch.

Titania What, wilt thou hear some music, my sweet love?

Bottom I have a reasonable good ear in music; let　　　30
　　us have the tongs and the bones.

Titania Or say, sweet love, what thou desir'st to eat.

Bottom Truly, a peck of provender; I could munch your
　　good dry oats. Methinks I have a great desire to
　　a bottle of hay: good hay, sweet hay, hath no　　　　35
　　fellow.

Titania I have a venturous fairy that shall seek
　　The squirrel's hoard, and fetch thee new nuts.

Bottom I had rather have a handful or two of dried peas.
　　But, I pray you, let none of your people stir me;　　　40
　　I have an exposition of sleep come upon me.

Titania Sleep thou, and I will wind thee in my arms.
　　Fairies, be gone, and be all ways away.
　　[Exeunt FAIRIES]
　　So doth the woodbine the sweet honeysuckle　　　　45
　　Gently entwist, the female ivy so
　　Enrings the barky fingers of the elm.
　　O, how I love thee! How I dote on thee!
　　[They sleep]
　　[OBERON advances. Enter PUCK]

23.　*Cavalery:* Cavaliere means "Sir" in Italian.

31.　*the tongs and the bones:* crude percussion instruments.

35.　*bottle:* bundle.

36.　*fellow:* equal.

41.　*exposition of:* Bottom's mistake for "disposition to."

45.　*woodbine:* convolvulus, bindweed.

47.　*Enrings:* encircles.

Oberon　Welcome, good Robin. Seest thou this sweet sight?
Her dotage now I do begin to pity;　　　　　　　　　　　50
For, meeting her of late behind the wood
Seeking sweet favours for this hateful fool,
I did upbraid her and fall out with her,
For she his hairy temples then had rounded
With coronet of fresh and fragrant flowers;　　　　　　55
And that same dew, which sometime on the buds
Was wont to swell like round and orient pearls,
Stood now within the pretty flow'rets' eyes,
Like tears that did their own disgrace bewail.
When I had at my pleasure taunted her,　　　　　　　60
And she in mild terms begged my patience,
I then did ask of her her changeling child,
Which straight she gave me, and her fairy sent
To bear him to my bower in fairy-land.
And now I have the boy, I will undo　　　　　　　　65
This hateful imperfection of her eyes.
And, gentle Puck, take this transformèd scalp
From off the head of this Athenian swain,
That he awaking when the other do,
May all to Athens back again repair,　　　　　　　70
And think no more of this night's accidents
But as the fierce vexation of a dream.
But first I will release the fairy queen.
[He drops the juice on TITANIA's eyelids]
Be as thou wast wont to be;
See as thou was wont to see.　　　　　　　　　75
Dian's bud o'er Cupid's flower
Hath such force and blessèd power.
Now, my Titania; wake you, my sweet queen.

Titania　*[waking]* My Oberon! what visions have I seen!
Methought I was enamoured of an ass.　　　　　80

Oberon　There lies your love.

68.　　*swain:* rustic.

70.　　*repair:* go.

72.　　*vexation:* affliction.

76.　　*Dian's bud:* the herb from which the juice is taken.

　　　　Cupid's flower: the pansy.

Titania How came these things to pass?
O, how mine eyes do loathe his visage now!

Oberon Silence awhile. Robin, take off this head.
Titania, music call, and strike more dead   85
Than common sleep of all these five the sense.

Titania Music, ho! music; such as charmeth sleep.
[Still music]

Puck Now when thou wak'st, with thine own fool's eyes peep.

Oberon Sound, music!
[The music changes]
Come, my queen, take hands with me,
And rock the ground whereon these sleepers be.   90
[They dance]
Now thou and I are new in amity,
And will to-morrow midnight solemnly
Dance in Duke Theseus' house triumphantly,
And bless it to all fair prosperity.
There shall the pairs of faithful lovers be   95
Wedded, with Theseus, all in jollity.

Puck Fairy king, attend and mark:
I do hear the morning lark.

Oberon Then, my queen, in silence sad,
Trip we after night's shade.   100
We the globe can compass soon,
Swifter than the wand'ring moon.

Titania Come, my lord; and in our flight,
Tell me how it came this night
That I sleeping here was found   105
With these mortals on the ground.
[Exeunt OBERON, TITANIA, and PUCK. Wind horns within.
Enter THESEUS, HIPPOLYTA, EGEUS, and Train]

Theseus Go, one of you, find out the forester;
For now our observation is performed;

---

83. *visage:* face.

SD. *Still music:* supernatural music.

97. *mark:* pay attention.

99. *sad:* sober.

SD. *Wind horns within:* hunting horns are sounded offstage.

SD. *Train:* attendants.

108. *observation:* observance (of the rites of May).

And since we have the vaward of the day,
My love shall hear the music of my hounds,   110
Uncouple in the western valley; go:
Despatch, I say, and find the forester.
[Exit an ATTENDANT]
We will, fair queen, up to the mountain's top,
And mark the musical confusion
Of hounds and echo in conjunction.   115

Hippolyta I was with Hercules and Cadmus once
When in a wood of Crete they bayed the bear
With hounds of Sparta: never did I hear
Such gallant chiding; for, besides the groves,
The skies, the fountains, every region near   120
Seemed all one mutual cry: I never heard
So musical a discord, such sweet thunder.

Theseus My hounds are bred out of the Spartan kind,
So flewed, so sanded; and their heads are hung
With ears that sweep away the morning dew;   125
Crook-kneeed and dew-lapped like Thessalian bulls;
Slow in pursuit, but matched in mouth like bells,
Each under each. A cry more tuneable
Was never hollaed to, nor cheered with horn,
In Crete, in Sparta, nor in Thessaly.   130
Judge when you hear. But, soft, what nymphs are these?

Egeus My lord, this is my daughter here asleep;
And this Lysander; this Demetrius is;
This Helena, old Nedar's Helena:
I wonder of their being here together.   135

Theseus No doubt they rose up early to observe
The rite of May; and, hearing our intent,
Came here in grace of our solemnity.
But speak, Egeus; is not this the day
That Hermia should give answer of her choice?   140

---

109. *vaward:* vanguard, first part.

113. *up:* go up.

116. *Hercules:* classical hero.
      Cadmus: legendary founder of Thebes.

118. *Sparta:* Spartan hounds were famous for their hunting prowess.

119. *chiding:* yelping.

124. *flewed:* with hanging chaps.
      sanded: sandy-colored.

126. *dew-lapped:* with hanging folds of skin at the throat.

128. *tuneable:* melodious.

138. *in grace of our solemnity:* to give honor to our marriage ceremony.

Egeus It is, my lord.

Theseus Go, bid the huntsmen wake them with their horns.
  [Horns, and shout within. DEMETRIUS, LYSANDER,
    HERMIA, and HELENA awake and start up]
  Good-morrow, friends. Saint Valentine is past;
  Begin these wood-birds but to couple now?

Lysander Pardon, my lord.
  [He and the rest kneel to THESEUS]

Theseus I pray you all, stand up.   145
  I know you two are rival enemies;
  How comes this gentle concord in the world,
  That hatred is so far from jealousy
  To sleep by hate, and fear no enmity?

Lysander My lord, I shall reply amazèdly,   150
  Half 'sleep, half waking; but as yet, I swear,
  I cannot truly say how I came here.
  But, as I think—for truly would I speak,
  And now I do bethink me, so it is—
  I came with Hermia hither. Our intent   155
  Was to be gone from Athens, where we might,
  Without the peril of the Athenian law—

Egeus Enough, enough, my lord; you have enough.
  I beg the law, the law upon his head.
  They would have stol'n away, they would, Demetrius,   160
  Thereby to have defeated you and me:
  You of your wife, and me of my consent,
  Of my consent that she should be your wife.

Demetrius My lord, fair Helen told me of their stealth,
  Of this their purpose hither to this wood;   165
  And I in fury hither followed them,
  Fair Helena in fancy following me.

144. *Begin these wood-birds but to couple now?:* Are these birds pairing up only now (as opposed to on St Valentine's day, February 14th, when birds were believed to choose their partners)?

148. *jealousy:* mistrust.

157. *Without:* beyond.

But, my good lord, I wot not by what power
(But by some power it is) my love to Hermia,
Melted as the snow seems to me now   170
As the remembrance of an idle gawd
Which in my childhood I did dote upon:
And all the faith, the virtue of my heart,
The object and the pleasure of mine eye,
Is only Helena. To her, my lord,   175
Was I betrothed ere I saw Hermia:
But like a sickness did I loathe this food;
But, as in health, come to my natural taste,
Now I do wish it, love it, long for it,
And will for evermore be true to it.   180

Theseus Fair lovers, you are fortunately met:
Of this discourse we more will hear anon.
Egeus, I will overbear your will;
For in the temple, by and by with us,
These couples shall eternally be knit.   185
And, for the morning now is something worn,
Our purposed hunting shall be set aside.
Away with us to Athens, three and three,
We'll hold a feast in great solemnity.
Come, Hippolyta.   190
[*Exeunt THESEUS, HIPPOLYTA, EGEUS, and Train*]

Demetrius These things seem small and undistinguishable,
Like far-off mountains turnèd into clouds.

Hermia Methinks I see these things with parted eye,
When every thing seems double.

Helena So methinks:
And I have found Demetrius like a jewel.   195
Mine own, and not mine own.

Demetrius It seems to me
That yet we sleep, we dream. Do not you think
The Duke was here, and bid us follow him?

168. *wot:* know.

171. *idle gawd:* worthless trinket.

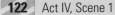

Hermia Yea, and my father.

Helena And Hippolyta.   200

Lysander And he did bid us follow to the temple.

Demetrius Why, then, we are awake: let's follow him;
And by the way let us recount our dreams.
[Exeunt]
[BOTTOM wakes]

Bottom When my cue comes, call me, and I will answer.
My next is 'Most fair Pyramus.' Heigh-ho! Peter   205
Quince! Flute, the bellows-mender! Snout, the
tinker! Starveling! God's my life, stol'n hence,
and left me asleep! I have had a most rare vision.
I have had a dream past the wit of man to say
what dream it was. Man is but an ass if he go   210
about to expound this dream. Methought I was
—there is no man can tell what. Methought I
—was—and methought I had—but man is but a
—patched fool if he will offer to say what me—
thought I had. The eye of man hath not heard,   215
the ear of man hath not seen; man's hand is not
able to taste, his tongue to conceive, nor his
heart to report, what my dream was. I will get
Peter Quince to write a ballad of this dream: it
shall be called 'Bottom's Dream', because it hath   220
no bottom; and I will sing it in the latter end of
a play, before the Duke. Peradventure, to
make it the more gracious, I shall sing it at her
death.

[Exit]

210. *go about:* sets about trying to.

214. *patched fool:* a fool (jester) wearing a suit of patches in contrasting colours.

220. *hath no bottom:* (1) has no foundation (2) is unfathomable.

222. *Peradventure:* perhaps.

223. *her:* Thisbe's.

COMMENTARY

The four lovers are all asleep unnoticed, and Titania, Bottom, and the fairies enter, followed and watched by Oberon. They do not see him. Titania invites Bottom to sit so that she can stroke and kiss his ass's head and ears. The sensuous and poetic language she uses intensifies the absurdity. She speaks in verse, while Bottom speaks in prose. The contrasting language emphasizes the mismatch between a royal fairy and a human buffoon with the head of an ass.

Bottom readily accepts this state of affairs, and this, too, is comic. He clearly finds it easy to issue instructions to his new fairy servants. He orders Cobweb to fetch him the "honey-bag" from a bee, issuing comically detailed instructions as to how he should do it. He addresses the fairies as if they are French or Italian gentlemen, as "Mounsieur Cobweb," "Mounsieur Mustardseed," and "Cavalery Peaseblossom."

Bottom and the fairies.
Clive Barda/PAL

Titania asks him if he wishes to hear some music; he asks to hear some played on the "tongs and the bones"—crude percussion instruments incapable of producing sounds of any delicacy or sweetness. When Titania asks him what he would like to eat, the most delightful food he can imagine is hay. Titania offers to send a fairy to get him some nuts from a squirrel's hoard, but he would rather have "a handful or two of dried peas." There is comedy in the contrast between the delicacies she could provide for him and the crudity of his requests. The absurdity is complete when they fall asleep in each other's arms, which they wind round one another as closely as honeysuckle and woodbine are entwined. Titania's last words before sleeping are magnificently ridiculous: "O, how I love thee! How I dote on thee!"

The scene is so absurd that Oberon, who has been secretly watching, feels sorry for Titania. He tells Puck that he recently met her as she was "[s]eeking sweet favours for this hateful fool" and that she readily gave him her Indian boy. His language is stately, and the delicacy with which he describes the dew on the flowers she had picked to decorate Bottom's head underlines the contrast between Titania's ethereal beauty and Bottom's bestial ugliness. He orders Puck to remove the ass's head from Bottom, while he undoes the spell on Titania. Once more, he speaks of how those who have been subjected to magic

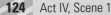

will wake to think they have experienced a dream. As he administers the juice, he utters the words of the spell in two short rhyming couplets.

Titania awakes with a start, thinking that she has been dreaming: "Methought I was enamoured of an ass!" Oberon shows her the sleeping Bottom, and she realizes that she really had fallen in love with him, though he is now repellent to her. Oberon asks her to conjure up music that will make Bottom and the four lovers sleep even more deeply, and the Fairy King and Queen dance around them as they sleep. Their dance together is a symbol that they are now happily reunited, and the music represents the harmony that they now enjoy and that the lovers will experience on awakening. This harmony and constancy is also reflected in the rhyme scheme of Oberon's speech: All eight lines end in a *y* sound. Now that the fairy kingdom is at peace with itself, the human world can fall back into proper order, too. Puck hears a lark sing, which means that morning must have come, and the fairies depart.

The sound of horns is heard. Theseus, Hippolyta, Egeus, and other courtiers arrive. They are out hunting. Theseus is proud of the "music" of his hounds and is happy that his "love," Hippolyta, is able to hear the sound of them. This is an image of musical harmony, which is picked up a few lines later when Theseus tells Hippolyta that they will be able to hear the hounds' cries echoing around the valley below them. The image is developed in the next couple of speeches. Hounds, of course, hunt together in packs, and their unity of purpose is reflected in the "sweet thunder" of their cries. This sustained imagery leaves us feeling that the bond between Theseus and Hippolyta is deep.

Oberon and Titania.
Ben Christopher/PAL

Egeus spots the four lovers lying asleep at their feet. Theseus remembers that this is the day by which Hermia must tell him whether she will choose to obey her father's order to marry Demetrius, to suffer death, or to live the life of a nun. The huntsmen blow their horns, and the lovers wake up with a start. Theseus is amazed to see them in such "gentle concord." Lysander begins to explain what he can of how they came to be together and at peace, but Egeus interrupts, demanding his punishment. Demetrius points out that his love for Hermia "[m]elted as the snow"—

though he does not know why—and that he now loves Helena, to whom he had been betrothed before the action of the play had begun. The four lovers are now happily matched. Seeing this, Theseus orders that Egeus' wishes be overruled and that the two couples should be married the next day in his own wedding ceremony.

Theseus, Hippolyta, Egeus, and their attendants depart, leaving the lovers amazed at what has happened. In another of the play's many references to sight and seeing, Demetrius says that everything appears strange to him, as if things were further away than they actually are; Hermia, too, sees things oddly, as if "everything seems double." Demetrius wonders whether they are awake or dreaming; but the others assure him that they really have just met the Duke, who has ordered them to follow him to the temple to be married—which they do. The last word uttered before they exit is "dreams," spoken by Demetrius. Once more, the audience is reminded of the dream-like qualities of this story.

Bottom is still on the stage and wakes up after they have left. He speaks in his customary prose, unlike the other characters in the scene. For a moment he thinks he is back where he was just before Puck gave him the ass's head; then he, too, thinks he has been dreaming: "I have had a most rare vision." (This is yet another reference to sight.) "I have had a dream past the wit of man to say what dream it was." The way he cannot bring himself to recount what he has "dreamed" is highly comic. His stumbling attempt to express its importance is ridiculous: He describes its grandeur in a clumsy and mistaken paraphrase of a well-known passage from the Bible. The text from St. Paul's First Letter to the Corinthians reads, "The eye hath not seen, and the ear hath not heard neither have entered into the heart of man the things which God hath prepared for them that love him." Bottom mixes up all the senses: "The eye of man hath not heard, the ear of man hath not seen," and so on. Just as ridiculously, he plans to recount his "dream" as a song in the play that he and the mechanicals are to put on for the Duke's wedding.

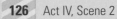
Act IV, Scene 2

Athens. A Room in QUINCE'S House. Bottom returns and the mechanicals rejoice.

ACT IV, SCENE 2

[Enter QUINCE, FLUTE, SNOUT, and STARVELING]

Quince Have you sent to Bottom's house? Is he come home yet?

Starveling He cannot be heard of. Out of doubt, he is transported.

Flute If he come not, then the play is marred; it goes   5
Not forward, doth it?

Quince It is not possible: you have not a man in all
Athens able to discharge Pyramus but he.

Flute No; he hath simply the best wit of any handi-
craft man in Athens.   10

Quince Yea, and the best person too: and he is a very
Paramour for a sweet voice.

Flute You must say paragon: a paramour is, God
bless us, a thing of naught.
[Enter SNUG the joiner]

Snug Masters, the Duke is coming from the temple;   15
and there is two or three lords and ladies more
married. If our sport had gone forward, we had
all been made men.

Flute O sweet bully Bottom! Thus hath he lost sixpence a day during his life. He could not have   20
'scaped sixpence a-day; and the Duke had not
given him sixpence a-day for playing Pyramus,
I'll be hanged; he would have deserved it: sixpence a-day in Pyramus, or nothing.
[Enter BOTTOM]

NOTES

4.   *transported:* carried away.

8.   *discharge:* perform.

14.   *naught:* wickedness.

17.   *we had all been made men:* we would
all have made our fortunes.

19.   *bully:* fine fellow.

      sixpence a day: an average wage for
a craftsman.

21.   *an:* if.

Bottom Where are these lads? Where are these hearts?   25

Quince Bottom! O most courageous day! O most happy hour!

Bottom Masters, I am to discourse wonders: but ask me
Not what; for if I tell you, I am not true Athenian. I will tell you everything, right as it fell
out.   30

Quince Let us hear, sweet Bottom.

Bottom Not a word of me. All that I will tell you is,
that the Duke hath dined. Get your apparel together; good strings to your beards, new rib-
bons to your pumps; meet presently at the pal-   35
ace; every man look over his part. For the short
and the long is, our play is preferred. In any
case, let Thisbe have clean linen; and let not him
that plays the lion pare his nails, for they shall
hang out for the lion's claws. And, most dear   40
actors, eat no onions nor garlick, for we are to
utter sweet breath; and I do not doubt but to
hear them say it is a sweet comedy. No more
words. Away, go, away!
[Exeunt]

25.   *hearts:* fine fellows.

34.   *strings to your beards:* tapes for false
      beards.

35.   *pumps:* light shoes.

      presently: immediately.

37.   *preferred:* recommended.

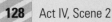

COMMENTARY

A day has passed. Quince, Flute, Snout, and Starveling are fretting because Bottom has disappeared and they cannot perform their play without him: "If he come not, then the play is marred." The audience realizes that this confidence in him is comically misplaced. Snug arrives, telling the others that the Duke's wedding ceremonies now include "two or three lords and ladies more married" and that on such an occasion their efforts would surely have been handsomely rewarded.

Bottom appears, brimming with confidence. He addresses the mechanicals warmly as "these lads" and "these hearts," and Quince speaks for all of them when he expresses his joy at Bottom's return. Another of the play's broken relationships has been put right. Bottom will tell them all about his adventures, but later. Now, they must quickly get themselves ready to put on their play. His appearance restores the flagging spirits of the mechanicals. The speech with which he ends the scene, a great list of instructions to his fellow players, moves the pace of the play up a gear after the dreaminess which marked the end of Act IV, Scene 1. For all his enthusiasm—and the mechanicals' readiness to be inspired by it—much of Bottom's advice is ridiculous. The players are to be sure that they eat no onions or garlic, so that their breath will reflect the sweetness of their "comedy," and Snug is not to cut his nails: Left long, they will look like the claws of the lion he is to represent.

NOTES

NOTES

NOTES

NOTES

A MIDSUMMER NIGHT'S DREAM

ACT V

Theseus *I will hear that play;*
For never anything can be amiss
When simpleness and duty tender it.
Go, bring them in: and take your places, ladies.

Act V, Scene 1

Athens. The palace of Theseus. The mechanicals perform their absurd play at the wedding celebrations. When the humans have gone to bed, the fairies arrive to bless the marriages. The play ends on a note of happy harmony.

ACT V, SCENE 1

[Enter THESEUS, HIPPOLYTA, PHILOSTRATE, Lords and Attendants]

Hippolyta 'Tis strange, my Theseus, that these lovers speak of.

Theseus More strange than true. I never may believe
These antique fables, nor these fairy toys.
Lovers and madmen have such seething brains,
Such shaping fantasies, that apprehend   5
More than cool reason ever comprehends.
The lunatic, the lover, and the poet
Are of imagination all compact:
One sees more devils than vast hell can hold;
That is the madman. The lover, all as frantic,   10
Sees Helen's beauty in a brow of Egypt.
The poet's eye, in a fine frenzy rolling,
Doth glance from heaven to earth, from earth to heaven;
And as imagination bodies forth
The forms of things unknown, the poet's pen   15
Turns them to shapes, and gives to airy nothing
A local habitation and a name.
Such tricks hath strong imagination,
That, if it would but apprehend some joy,
It comprehends some bringer of that joy;   20
Or in the night, imagining some fear,
How easy is a bush supposed a bear?

Hippolyta But all the story of the night told over,
And all their minds transfigured so together,
More witnesseth than fancy's images,   25

NOTES

3. *fairy toys:* idle fairy tales.

5. *apprehend:* seize on.

6. *comprehends:* understands.

8. *compact:* composed.

11. *in a brow of Egypt:* in an Egyptian (i.e., dark-skinned) face.

12. *frenzy:* madness.

14. *bodies forth:* embodies.

19. *apprehend:* conceives.

20. *comprehends:* includes.

And grows to something of great constancy;
But, howsoever, strange and admirable.
[Enter LYSANDER, DEMETRIUS, HERMIA, and HELENA]

Theseus Here come the lovers, full of joy and mirth.
Joy, gentle friends! Joy and fresh days of love
Accompany your hearts!

Lysander More than to us   30
Wait in your royal walks, your board, your bed!

Theseus Come now; what masques, what dances shall we have,
To wear away this long age of three hours
Between our after-supper and bed-time?
Where is our usual manager of mirth?   35
What revels are in hand? Is there no play
To ease the anguish of a torturing hour?
Call Philostrate.

Philostrate Here, mighty Theseus.

Theseus Say, what abridgment have you for this evening?
What masque? What music? How shall we beguile   40
The lazy time, if not with some delight?

Philostrate There is a brief how many sports are ripe;
Make choice of which your highness will see first.
[Giving a paper]

Theseus *[Reads]* 'The battle with the Centaurs, to be sung
By an Athenian eunuch to the harp.'   45
We'll none of that; that have I told my love,
In glory of my kinsman Hercules.
'The riot of the tipsy Bacchanals,
Tearing the Thracian singer in their rage.'
That is an old device, and it was played   50

27.   *admirable:* marvelous.

32.   *masques:* spectacular court entertainments with masked participants.

35.   *manager of mirth:* official in charge of entertainments at court.

36.   *revels:* amusements.

39.   *abridgment:* (1) short version of a play (2) something to make the time seem short.

42.   *brief:* summary.

44.   *Centaurs:* in classical mythology, creatures that are half man and half horse.

45.   *eunuch:* castrated man (thus with a high voice).

48.   *Bacchanals:* female followers of Bacchus, god of wine.

49.   *Thracian:* from the northernmost part of Greece.

50.   *device:* show.

When I from Thebes came last a conqueror.
'The thrice three Muses mourning for the death
Of learning, late deceased in beggary.'
That is some satire, keen and critical,
Not sorting with a nuptial ceremony.　　　　　　　55
'A tedious brief scene of young Pyramus
And his love Thisbe; very tragical mirth.'
Merry and tragical? Tedious and brief?
That is hot ice and wondrous strange black snow.
How shall we find the concord of this discord?　　60

Philostrate A play there is, my lord, some ten words long,
Which is as 'brief' as I have known a play;
But by ten words, my lord, it is too long,
Which makes it 'tedious'. For in all the play
There is not one word apt, one player fitted.　　　65
And 'tragical', my noble lord, it is,
For Pyramus therein doth kill himself;
Which when I saw rehearsed, I must confess,
Made mine eyes water; but more 'merry' tears
The passion of loud laughter never shed.　　　　70

Theseus What are they that do play it?

Philostrate Hard-handed men that work in Athens here,
Which never laboured in their minds till now;
And now have toiled their unbreathed memories
With this same play against your nuptial.　　　　75

Theseus And we will hear it.

Philostrate No, my noble lord,
It is not for you: I have heard it over,
And it is nothing, nothing in the world,
Unless you can find sport in their intents,
Extremely stretched, and conned with cruel pain,　　80
To do you service.

52.　*Muses:* goddesses of literature, music, and dance.

54.　*satire:* a play mocking vices.

55.　*sorting with:* appropriate for.

70.　*passion:* strong feeling.

74.　*toiled:* made tired with labor.
　　unbreathed: unpractised.

75.　*against:* in preparation for.

80.　*conned:* learned.

Theseus I will hear that play;
  For never anything can be amiss
  When simpleness and duty tender it.
  Go, bring them in: and take your places, ladies.
  [Exit PHILOSTRATE]

Hippolyta I love not to see wretchedness o'er-charged,   85
  And duty in his service perishing.

Theseus Why, gentle sweet, you shall see no such thing.

Hippolyta He says they can do nothing in this kind.

Theseus The kinder we, to give them thanks for nothing.
  Our sport shall be to take what they mistake;   90
  And what poor duty cannot do,
  Noble respect takes it in might, not merit.
  Where I have come, great clerks have purposed
  To greet me with premeditated welcomes,
  Where I have seen them shiver and look pale,   95
  Make periods in the midst of sentences,
  Throttle their practised accent in their fears,
  And, in conclusion, dumbly have broke off,
  Not paying me a welcome. Trust me, sweet,
  Out of this silence yet I picked a welcome;   100
  And in the modesty of fearful duty
  I read as much as from the rattling tongue
  Of saucy and audacious eloquence.
  Love, therefore, and tongue-tied simplicity
  In least speak most to my capacity.   105
  [Enter PHILOSTRATE]

Philostrate So please your grace, the Prologue is addressed.

Theseus Let him approach.
  [Flourish of trumpets. Enter QUINCE, as PROLOGUE]

---

83. *simpleness:* artless sincerity.

85. *wretchedness o'er-charged:* low people overburdened.

90. *take:* accept, understand.

92. *Noble respect:* magnanimous consideration.

93. *clerks:* scholars.

94. *premeditated:* prepared, thought out in advance.

96. *Make periods:* i.e., come to an inappropriate stop.

101. *modesty:* deference.

105. *to my capacity:* as far as I can judge.

106. *Prologue:* the character who reads the introduction.
  addressed: (dressed and) ready.

Quince *(as Prologue)* 'If we offend, it is with our good will.
  That you should think, we come not to offend,
  But with good will. To show our simple skill,   110
  That is the true beginning of our end.
  Consider then, we come but in despite.
  We do not come, as minding to content you,
  Our true intent is. All for your delight
  We are not here. That you should here repent you,   115
  The actors are at hand: and, by their show,
  You shall know all that you are like to know,'

Theseus This fellow doth not stand upon points.

Lysander He hath rid his prologue like a rough colt; he
  Knows not the stop. A good moral, my lord: it   120
  is not enough to speak, but to speak true.

Hippolyta Indeed he hath played on this prologue like a
  Child on a recorder; a sound, but not in government.

Theseus
  His speech was like a tangled chain; nothing   125
  impaired, but all disordered. Who is next?
  [Enter with a Trumpeter before them BOTTOM as PYRAMUS,
    FLUTE as THISBE, SNOUT as WALL, STARVELING as
    MOONSHINE, and SNUG as LION]

Quince *(as Prologue)* Gentles, perchance you wonder at this
  show;
  But wonder on, till truth make all things plain.
  This man is Pyramus, if you would know;   130
  This beauteous lady Thisbe is, certain.
  This man, with lime and rough-cast, doth present
  Wall, that vile Wall which did these lovers sunder;
  And through Wall's chink, poor souls, they are content

---

110. *But:* except.

112. *in despite:* in contempt.

116. *show:* appearance; also refers to the dumb-show that follows.

118. *stand upon points:* bother with details.

120. *the stop:* full stop, period.

124. *in government:* under control.

131. *certain:* (The second syllable is stressed.)

132. *present:* represent.

To whisper, at the which let no man wonder.   135

This man, with lanthorn, dog, and bush of thorn,

Presenteth Moonshine; for, if you will know,

By moonshine did these lovers think no scorn

To meet at Ninus' tomb, there, there to woo.

This grisly beast, which Lion hight by name,   140

The trusty Thisbe, coming first by night,

Did scare away, or rather did affright;

And as she fled, her mantle she did fall,

Which Lion vile with bloody mouth did stain.

Anon comes Pyramus, sweet youth, and tall,   145

And finds his trusty Thisbe's mantle slain;

Whereat with blade, with bloody blameful blade,

He bravely broached his boiling bloody breast;

And Thisbe, tarrying in mulberry shade,

His dagger drew, and died. For all the rest,   150

Let Lion, Moonshine, Wall, and lovers twain,

At large discourse while here they do remain.

[Exeunt QUINCE, BOTTOM, FLUTE, SNUG, and
    STARVELING]

Theseus I wonder if the lion be to speak.

Demetrius No wonder, my lord: one lion may, when many asses

do.   155

Snout *(as Wall)* In this same interlude it doth befall

That I, one Snout by name, present a wall;

And such a wall as I would have you think

That had in it a crannied hole or chink,

Through which the lovers, Pyramus and Thisbe,   160

Did whisper often, very secretly.

This loam, this rough-cast, and this stone, doth show

That I am that same wall; the truth is so.

And this the cranny is, right and sinister,

Through which the fearful lovers are to whisper.   165

Theseus Would you desire lime and hair to speak better?

---

136. *lanthorn:* lantern.

139. *woo:* go courting.

140. *hight:* (is) called.

143. *fall:* i.e., let fall.

145. *tall:* brave and handsome.

148. *broached:* opened by piercing (as one would open a cask of wine).

156. *interlude:* play.

162. *stone:* (carried by Snout to show he represents Wall).

164. *sinister:* left (The accent is on the second syllable.)

Demetrius It is the wittiest partition that ever I heard
discourse, my lord.
[Enter BOTTOM as PYRAMUS.]

Theseus Pyramus draws near the wall; silence.   170

Bottom *(as Pyramus)* O grim-looked night! O night with hue
so black! O night, which ever art when day is not!
O night, O night, alack, alack, alack,
I fear my Thisbe's promise is forgot!
And thou, O wall, O sweet, O lovely wall,   175
That stand'st between her father's ground and mine;
Thou wall, O wall, O sweet and lovely wall,
Show me thy chink, to blink through with mine eyne.
[WALL holds up his fingers]
Thanks, courteous wall: Jove shield thee well for this!
But what see I? No Thisbe do I see.   180
O wicked wall, through whom I see no bliss,
Cursed be thy stones for thus deceiving me!

Theseus The wall, methinks, being sensible, should curse again.

Bottom *(as Pyramus)* No, in truth, sir, he should not. 'Deceiving
me' is   185
Thisbe's cue: she is to enter now, and I am to
spy her through the wall. You shall see it will
fall pat as I told you. Yonder she comes.
[Enter THISBE]

Flute *(as Thisbe)* O wall, full often hast thou heard my moans, 190
For parting my fair Pyramus and me:
My cherry lips have often kissed thy stones:
Thy stones with lime and hair knit up in thee.

167.   *partition:* wall.

178.   *eyne:* eyes.

179.   *Jove:* Jupiter, chief of Roman gods.

184.   *being sensible:* having feelings.

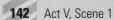

Bottom *(as Pyramus)* I see a voice; now will I to the chink,
To spy an I can hear my Thisbe's face.   195
Thisbe!

Flute *(as Thisbe)* My love! Thou art my love, I think.

Bottom *(as Pyramus)* Think what thou wilt, I am thy lover's
grace;
And like Limander am I trusty still.

Flute *(as Thisbe)* And I like Helen, till the fates me kill.   200

Bottom *(as Pyramus)* Not Shafalus to Procrus was so true.

Flute *(as Thisbe)* As Shafalus to Procrus, I to you.

Bottom *(as Pyramus)* O, kiss me through the hole of this vile wall.

Flute *(as Thisbe)* I kiss the wall's hole, not your lips at all.

Bottom *(as Pyramus)* Wilt thou at Ninny's tomb meet me
straightway?   205

Flute *(as Thisbe)* Tide life, tide death, I come without delay.
[Exeunt Bottom and Flute severally]

Snout *(as Wall)* Thus have I, wall, my part dischargèd so;
And, being done, thus Wall away doth go.
[Exit]

Theseus Now is the mural down between the two neighbours.

Demetrius No remedy, my lord, when walls are so wilful to   210
Hear without warning.

Hippolyta This is the silliest stuff that ever I heard.

---

199. *Limander:* malapropism for Leander, a classical hero.

201. *Shafalus to Procrus:* a similar mistake; Cephalus accidentally killed his wife, Procris.

206. *tide:* come.

SD: *severally:* i.e., in different directions.

210. *wilful:* willing.

Theseus The best in this kind are but shadows; and the
worst are no worse, if imagination amend them.   215

Hippolyta It must be your imagination then, and not theirs.

Theseus If we imagine no worse of them than they of
themselves, they may pass for excellent men.
[Enter SNUG as LION and STARVELING as MOONSHINE]
Here come two noble beasts in, a moon and a   220
lion.

Snug *(as Lion)* You, ladies, you, whose gentle hearts do fear
The smallest monstrous mouse that creeps on floor,
May now, perchance, both quake and tremble here,
When lion rough in wildest rage doth roar.   225
Then know that I, one Snug the joiner, am
A lion fell, nor else no lion's dam:
For, if I should as lion come in strife
Into this place, 'twere pity on my life.

Theseus A very gentle beast, and of a good conscience.   230

Demetrius The very best at a beast, my lord, that e'er I saw.

Lysander This lion is a very fox for his valour.

Theseus True; and a goose for his discretion.   235

Demetrius Not so, my lord; for his valour cannot carry his
discretion, and the fox carries the goose.

Theseus His discretion, I am sure, cannot carry his valour; for
the goose carries not the fox. It is well;   240
leave it to his discretion, and let us listen to the
moon.

214. *shadows:* dreams, illusions.

227. *fell:* fierce.

      dam: female parent.

231. *best at a beast:* a pun.

234. *fox:* associated with slyness.

235. *goose:* associated with stupidity.

Starveling *(as Moonshine)* This lanthorn doth the hornèd moon
　present:

Demetrius He should have worn the horns on his head.　　　245

Theseus He is no crescent, and his horns are invisible
　Within the circumference.

Starveling *(as Moonshine)* This lanthorn doth the hornèd moon
　present;
　Myself the man i' the moon do seem to be.

Theseus This is the greatest error of all the rest: the man　　250
　should be put into the lantern. How is it else
　the man i' the moon?

Demetrius He dares not come there for the candle: for, you
　see, it is already in snuff.

Hippolyta I am aweary of this moon: would he would　　255
　change!

Theseus It appears, by his small light of discretion, that
　he is in the wane: but yet, in courtesy, in all rea-
　son, we must stay the time.

Lysander Proceed, moon.　　　260

Starveling *(as Moonshine)* All that I have to say, is to tell you
　　that the lan-
　tern is the moon; I, the man i' the moon; this
　thorn-bush, my thorn-bush; and this dog, my dog.

Demetrius Why, all these should be in the lantern; for all　　265
　these are in the moon. But silence; here comes
　Thisbe.

245. *on his head:* like a cuckold—a man who is said to have horns on his head that everyone else can see, but he can't. (A cuckold is a man whose wife is having an affair that everyone knows about except him.)

246. *crescent:* (The joke is that Starveling is thin.)

254. *in snuff:* (1) needing to be snuffed out (2) angry.

258. *in all reason:* as is only reasonable.

[Enter FLUTE as THISBE]

Flute *(as Thisbe)* This is old Ninny's tomb. Where is my love?

Snug *(as Lion)* Oh!
[LION roars. THISBE runs off]

Demetrius Well roared, lion.   270

Theseus Well run, Thisbe.

Hippolyta Well shone, moon. Truly, the moon shines with a
  good grace.

Theseus Well moused, lion.

Demetrius And so comes Pyramus.

Lysander And then the lion vanishes.   275
  [LION worries THISBE'S Mantle, and exits]
  [Enter BOTTOM as PYRAMUS]

Bottom *(as Pyramus)* Sweet moon, I thank thee for thy sunny
  beams;
  I thank thee, moon, for shining now so bright:
  For, by thy gracious golden, glittering gleams,
  I trust to take of truest Thisbe's sight.   280
  But stay—O spite!
  But mark, poor knight,
  What dreadful dole is here!
  Eyes, do you see?
  How can it be?   285
  O dainty duck! O dear!
  Thy mantle good,
  What! stained with blood?
  Approach, ye furies fell!
  O fates! come, come,   290
  Cut thread and thrum,
  Quail, rush, conclude, and quell!

273. *moused:* played like a mouse.

283. *dole:* cause for sorrow.

289. *furies:* goddesses of vengeance.

291. *thread and thrum:* parts of cloth. The Fates were three goddesses who spun, drew out, and cut the thread of life.

292. *Quail:* destroy.

quell: kill.

Theseus This passion, and the death of a dear friend, would go near to make a man look sad.

293. *passion:* (1) suffering (2) passionate outburst.

Hippolyta Beshrew my heart, but I pity the man. 295

Bottom *(as Pyramus)* O wherefore, nature, didst thou lions frame?
Since lion vile hath here deflowered my dear;
Which is—no, no—which was the fairest dame
That lived, that loved, that liked, that looked with cheer.
Come, tears, confound; 300
Out, sword, and wound
The pap of Pyramus:
Ay, that left pap,
Where heart doth hop:
Thus die I, thus, thus, thus. 305
[He stabs himself]
Now am I dead,
Now am I fled;
My soul is in the sky:
Tongue, lose thy light!
Moon, take thy flight! 310
[Exit STARVELING]
Now die, die, die, die, die.
[He dies]

297. *deflowered:* perhaps a mistake for "devoured."

Demetrius No die, but an ace, for him; for he is but one.

312. *die:* one of pair of dice.

ace: pronounced with a short "a."

Lysander Less than an ace, man; for he is dead; he is nothing. 315

Theseus With the help of a surgeon he might yet recover and prove an ass.

316. *ass:* pun on "ace."

Hippolyta How chance moonshine is gone before Thisbe comes back and finds her lover?

Theseus She will find him by starlight. Here she comes;   320
And her passion ends the play.
[Enter FLUTE as THISBE]

Hippolyta Methinks she should not use a long one for such
A Pyramus; I hope she will be brief.

Demetrius A mote will turn the balance, which Pyramus,
Which Thisbe, is the better: he for a man, God   325
warrant us; she for a woman, God bless us.

Lysander She hath spied him already with those sweet
eyes.

Demetrius And thus she means, videlicet—   330

Flute *(as Thisbe)* Asleep, my love?
What, dead, my dove?
O Pyramus, arise,
Speak, speak. Quite dumb?
Dead, dead? A tomb   335
Must cover thy sweet eyes.
These lily lips,
This cherry nose,
These yellow cowslip cheeks,
Are gone, are gone: 340
Lovers, make moan!
His eyes were green as leeks.
O Sisters Three,
Come, come to me,
With hands as pale as milk;   345
Lay them in gore,
Since you have shore
With shears his thread of silk.
Tongue, not a word:
Come, trusty sword;   350
Come, blade, my breast imbrue;

321. *passion:* passionate speech.

324. *mote:* tiny speck of dust.

326. *warrant:* preserve.

330. *means:* (1) signifies (2) laments.
videlicet: as you may see.

343. *Sisters Three:* the Fates.

347. *shore:* shorn.

351. *imbrue:* pierce.

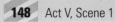

[Stabs herself]
And farewell, friends:
Thus Thisbe ends;
Adieu, adieu, adieu.
[Dies]

Theseus Moonshine and Lion are left to bury the dead.   355

Demetrius Ay, and Wall too.

Bottom No, I assure you; the wall is down that parted
their fathers. Will it please you to see the epilogue, or to hear a Bergomask dance between   360
two of our company?
[BOTTOM and FLUTE stand up]

Theseus No epilogue, I pray you; for your play needs no
excuse. Never excuse; for when the players are
all dead there need none to be blamed. Marry,
if he that writ it had played Pyramus, and   365
hanged himself in Thisbe's garter, it would have
been a fine tragedy: and so it is, truly; and very
notably discharged. But come, your Bergo-
mask; let your epilogue alone.
*[The company return; then two of them dance, then exeunt
   Bottom, Flute, and their fellows]*
The iron tongue of midnight hath told twelve: 370
Lovers, to bed; 'tis almost fairy time.
I fear we shall out-sleep the coming morn,
As much as we this night have overwatched.
This palpable-gross play hath well beguiled
The heavy gait of night. Sweet friends, to bed.   375
A fortnight hold we this solemnity,
In nightly revels and new jollity.
[Exeunt]
[Enter PUCK carrying a broom]

Puck Now the hungry lion roars,
And the wolf behowls the moon;

360. *Bergomask:* clownish dance.

364. *Marry:* by (the Virgin) Mary—a light oath.

370. *iron tongue:* clapper (of a bell).

373. *overwatched:* stayed up longer than our appointed time.

374. *palpable-gross:* obviously rough.

Whilst the heavy ploughman snores,   380
All with weary task fordone.
Now the wasted brands do glow,
Whilst the scritch-owl, scritching loud,
Puts the wretch that lies in woe
In remembrance of a shroud.   385
Now it is the time of night
That the graves, all gaping wide,
Every one lets forth its sprite,
In the church-way paths to glide:
And we fairies, that do run   390
By the triple Hecate's team
From the presence of the sun,
Following darkness like a dream,
Now are frolic; not a mouse
Shall disturb this hallowed house: 395
I am sent with broom before,
To sweep the dust behind the door.
[Enter OBERON and TITANIA, with all their Train]

Oberon Through the house give glimmering light,
By the dead and drowsy fire:
Every elf and fairy sprite   400
Hop as light as bird from briar,
And this ditty, after me,
Sing and dance it trippingly.

Titania First, rehearse your song by rote,
To each word a warbling note;   405
Hand in hand, with fairy grace,
Will we sing, and bless this place.
[Song and Dance]

Oberon Now, until the break of day,
Through this house each fairy stray,
To the best bride-bed will we,   410
Which by us shall blessed be;
And the issue there create

---

380. *heavy:* with weariness.

381. *fordone:* tired out.

382. *wasted:* burnt-out.

385. *shroud:* cloth in which a body is wrapped before burial.

388. *sprite:* spirit, ghost.

391. *triple Hecate's team:* moon goddess's chariot horses. Hecate had roles on earth, in the underworld, and in the heavens.

394. *frolic:* merry.

398. *glimmering light:* The fairies have lighted tapers in their headbands.

404. *rehearse:* repeat.

412. *the issue there create:* the children created therein.

Ever shall be fortunate.
So shall all the couples three
Ever true in loving be;   415
And the blots of Nature's hand
Shall not in their issue stand:

417. *in their issue:* their children.

Never mole, hare-lip, nor scar,
Nor mark prodigious, such as are

419. *mark prodigious:* ominous birthmark.

Despisèd in nativity,   420
Shall upon their children be.
With this field-dew consecrate,

422. *consecrate:* consecrated.

Every fairy take his gait,
And each several chamber bless

424. *several:* separate.

Through this palace, with sweet peace;   425
E'er shall it in safety rest,
And the owner of it blest.
Trip away:
Make no stay:
Meet me all by break of day.
[Exeunt all but PUCK]

Puck If we shadows have offended,   430
Think but this, and all is mended,

430. *shadows:* delusive appearances.

That you have but slumbered here
While these visions did appear.
And this weak and idle theme,
No more yielding but a dream,   435
Gentles, do not reprehend;

435. *No more yielding but:* producing nothing more than.

436. *Gentles:* ladies and gentleman.

If you pardon, we will mend.
And, as I am an honest Puck,

437. *mend:* do better.

If we have unearned luck
Now to 'scape the serpent's tongue,   440
We will make amends ere long;

440. *serpent's tongue:* i.e., snake-like hisses of disapproval.

Else the Puck a liar call:
So, good night unto you all.
Give me your hands, if we be friends,

444. *Give me your hands:* clap.

And Robin shall restore amends.   445
[Exit]

445. *restore amends:* give satisfaction in return.

COMMENTARY

The play has come full circle. We are in the Athenian court, just as we began, with two exceptions: The brittle old character Egeus is not there to spoil the general air of celebration, and all the broken relationships have now been mended. In that sense, the action of the play has been completed. The promised wedding of Theseus and Hippolyta has taken place. Oberon and Titania are reconciled. The four young lovers are happily married. Bottom is reunited with his friends, and the only expectation yet to be fulfilled is the performance of the play-within-a-play. But that does not mean that the last scene is unimportant: far from it.

It is night; supper has ended, and the moon is shining. Theseus and Hippolyta talk over the extraordinary stories they have been hearing from the four lovers. To Hippolyta, their tales are "strange;" Theseus just doesn't believe them. He says that lovers are like poets and lunatics: They have super-charged imaginations. Madmen see more devils than there are in hell. A man in love thinks that the woman he loves is as beautiful as Helen of Troy (generally believed to be the most beautiful woman ever born) just because she has a dusky complexion. Poets roll their eyes from heaven to earth and back again and then write down what their frenzied imaginations produce. Hippolyta, however, believes that there is significance in the stories the lovers have told and that there is something altogether wonderful about them.

The lovers enter. Whatever doubts Theseus may have about the truth of their stories, he greets them happily. The celebratory mood is inescapable: Shakespeare uses the word "joy" three times in Theseus's two-and-a-half-line speech. Theseus calls for his "usual manager of mirth," Philostrate, and asks him what entertainment he has arranged for the rest of the evening. Philostrate shows

him a list of the diversions that have been prepared. He rejects the first three as inappropriate to the happy mood of the occasion and asks Philostrate about the last on the list, which is described as "Merry and tragical" and "Tedious and brief." He wonders how anything can have such contradictory qualities; such descriptions make as much sense as saying that there is such a thing as "hot ice."

He then asks a question that goes to the heart of *A Midsummer Night's Dream*: "How shall we find the concord of this discord?" Throughout the play, Shakespeare has repeatedly used *antithesis* (the placing of opposite ideas beside each other) to signify disunity and division. In order for the play to end happily—which, as a comedy, it must—those opposites must be reconciled, that division and disunity replaced by harmony and unity. This has already happened in the main plot lines that make up *A Midsummer Night's Dream*, but we are yet to see how the absurd contradictions of the play-within-the-play can be reconciled. The prospect of the failure of the mechanicals' performance of *Pyramus and Thisbe* has been hanging over the audience from the beginning. It has been obvious since its ridiculous title was first mentioned (in Act I, Scene 2) that this "most lamentable comedy" would be a flop. If *A Midsummer Night's Dream* is to end happily, Shakespeare must somehow achieve the impossible: *Pyramus and Thisbe* must be some kind of success.

Philostrate attempts to dissuade Theseus from calling for the mechanicals' play to be performed. He has seen it in rehearsal and admits that he cried at the death of Pyramus—tears of laughter, because it was so ridiculous. Theseus nevertheless insists that he will see it, "For never anything can be amiss / When simpleness and duty tender it." Hippolyta tries to persuade him to change his

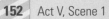

mind: Seeing simple people biting off more than they can chew will be an embarrassment. But Theseus is determined to have the play performed. At times, even great scholars have been so nervous in his presence that they have stumbled and broken down in making formal speeches of welcome to him. He wants to enjoy the simple honesty of the mechanicals' attempts to please him. "Trust me," he says to Hippolyta.

Dance of Apollo and the Muses by Baldassare Peruzzi
Arte&Immagini srl/CORBIS

A grand fanfare announces the entry of Quince to recite the prologue to the play. He pauses in all the wrong places and garbles the text. Theseus, Lysander, and Hippolyta all notice this and comment on it. Trumpets sound again, and Bottom (as Pyramus), Flute (as Thisbe), Snout (as Wall), Starveling (as Moonshine), and Snug (as Lion) all enter. Quince (as Prologue) introduces the characters to the audience. Quince tells the audience what will happen, removing any possibility of tension or excitement. The story of their play is that Pyramus and Thisbe are lovers who live in neighboring houses separated by a wall. There is a small hole in the wall through which they converse. They arrange to meet one night at Ninus' tomb, but a lion appears and frightens away Thisbe, who drops her mantle as she runs. The lion touches the mantle with his bloodstained mouth, and when Pyramus arrives, he sees the mantle and assumes that Thisbe is dead, so he kills himself. Thisbe finds his body and kills herself, too.

The joke is not just that Quince gives away the plot, but also that he does so in a speech of such ridiculously inflated style, in which Shakespeare mocks the work of some other playwrights. The Prologue's description of the death of Pyramus is full of choking *alliteration* (repetition of consonant sounds): "Whereat with **b**lade, with **b**loody **b**lameful **b**lade, / He **b**ravely **b**roached his **b**oiling **b**loody **b**reast." These fantastically puffed-up words are followed by a description of the death of Thisbe which is so matter-of-fact that the contrast is hilarious: "And Thisbe, tarrying in the mulberry shade, / His dagger drew, and died." The literary term for a clash of tone between the high and the low like this is *bathos*. Bathos is what makes the play-within-a-play so funny.

When the prologue is over, all the players leave except Snout, who explains that he represents the wall that separates the lovers. Bottom re-enters, playing Pyramus. His speech, too, is ridiculously grandiose. He addresses night and the wall directly (a device known as *apostrophe*), but he has nothing to say to them. He calls night "black" and tells it that it is always around when day is not. The verses he speaks are nearly all padding—terrible style with little or no content. Words are used or repeated just to fill up the metrical pattern in the lines, as in "O night, O night, alack, alack, alack!" and "thou, O wall, O sweet O lovely wall." When he curses the wall because he can't see Thisbe through it, Theseus remarks that as the wall is actually a human being, it might curse back in reply. Bottom drops out of character (and into his own prose) to explain to Theseus what is happening. This is high comedy: Bottom clearly has not the faintest understanding of how to create or maintain the magical reality of drama.

Flute (as Thisbe) enters, and the two lovers exchange lines in which they compare their devotion to each other to that of heroes of classical mythology (whose names they get comically wrong). They arrange to meet at Ninus' tomb, which Bottom incorrectly pronounces "Ninny's." Snout (as Wall) announces that his part is now finished, and he exits. Theseus and Hippolyta exchange remarks about what they have seen. Hippolyta says, "This is the silliest stuff that ever I heard." Theseus replies that even the best plays are only "shadows," and they can make up for the deficiencies of the worst plays by using their imagination. The use of the word "shadows" (which suggests visions and illusions) reminds the audience of the dream world of the fairies and the dreamlike nature of A *Midsummer Night's Dream* itself.

Snug enters to tell the ladies that, although he is playing a lion, they must not be afraid of him. This is another comic variation on Shakespeare's theme of appearance and reality, of things not being what they seem. Theseus, Demetrius, and Lysander exchange witty remarks about him. Their banter is a sign of their friendship and ease in each other's company. They joke about the lion's very un-lionly qualities and compare him to a fox and a goose, cowardly and stupid creatures.

Starveling enters and begins to explain that he represents the light of the moon, but he stops speaking when his audience begins to talk about him. He starts and stops again and finally loses his temper and tells them in his own words (in prose) that the long and the short of it is that "the lantern is the moon; I the man i' the moon; this thorn-bush, my thorn-bush; and this dog, my dog." The Athenian audience clearly enjoys the absurdity of all this, and their enjoyment increases when the lion enters and roars, Thisbe runs off, and the lion tears her mantle.

Bottom (as Pyramus) returns and addresses the moon, thanking it for providing light by which he hopes to see Thisbe. Again, his speech includes overpowering alliteration—"**g**racious **g**olden, **g**littering **g**leams"—in which the words have little to contribute beyond the fact that they begin with the same letter. The rhythm changes dramatically when he sees Thisbe's bloodstained fallen mantle, but instead of heightening the tension, the short lines in a different rhyme scheme bring us down with a bump. This kind of verse would be more appropriate to the telling of a comic story with a punch line. The grand words employed here just seem ridiculous, particularly with the line "O dainty duck, O dear!" in the midst of them, another example of bathos.

Bottom (as Pyramus) now addresses Nature and his tears before addressing his sword, with which he stabs himself. His drawn-out death is accompanied by an unconsciously comic commentary concluding with the repeated word "die." Bottom is, of course, a ham actor, and the real actor playing the part of Bottom has marvelous opportunities here to ham it up and tease the real audience, which has no way of knowing how many times "die" will be repeated and when the death scene will actually stop.

The death of Thisbe is almost as ridiculous and is preceded by a speech in the same inappropriately lilting pattern as that used by Pyramus. Her grieving description of her lover's dead body as having a "cherry nose" and eyes that were "green as leeks" is comically inappropriate, and her death line—"Adieu, adieu, adieu."—is all the funnier for fitting into the metrical pattern of her speech. The two dead lovers then leap to their feet, not lingering for dramatic effect, and Bottom confusedly asks the Duke if he would like to "see the epilogue, or to hear a Bergomask dance." Theseus settles for the dance, which is performed. As before, the dance symbolizes order and harmony: For all its absurdity, the performance of the play-within-the-play has ended happily, because the performers and their audience have enjoyed it, albeit for different reasons. The clock strikes midnight, and Theseus declares that it is time for them to go to bed, for "'tis almost fairy time."

Crude as it was, the play of *Pyramus and Thisbe* has whiled away the evening happily. That was the purpose of the play, so it has been a success. The unconscious comedy has caught the spirit of the occasion; indeed, only at a happy time like this, with an audience in such a celebratory and good-natured frame of mind, could the play have been well received.

The mortals exit, and Puck enters, carrying the broom with which he is often depicted. He gives a richly poetic description of night, quickly changing the atmosphere to one of eerie expectation and darkness. Oberon, Titania, and the fairies enter, instantly bringing light and driving away Puck's fearful nighttime images. They sing and dance together, a sign of the harmony that now exists in the fairy kingdom, which is reflected in the happiness now found in the mortal world. They bless the married couples so that their children will be lucky and unblemished by deformities, then they all exit, leaving Puck alone on the stage.

Puck addresses the audience directly, in a speech that rounds off the play with an invitation for applause and is something much more besides. He asks the audience to think of what they have just experienced in the theater as if it had been a dream, and he speaks of himself and the other characters as "shadows"—illusions. On one level, Puck is speaking in character and bridging the gap between the fairy and mortal world by speaking directly to the human beings in the audience. But on another level, he is speaking as an actor—one of the troupe of real men that has acted out the play of *A Midsummer Night's Dream* for the entertainment of real men and women.

One key element within *A Midsummer Night's Dream* has been the effect of magic. When the actor playing Puck stands alone on the stage talking to the audience, he is necessarily reminding them that there is another kind of magic—the magic of the theatre, through which they have been swept up and made to believe for a short while in the story that has been acted out for them. *A Midsummer Night's Dream* is an illusion created by Shakespeare, which contains illusions created by its characters, who ultimately see life straight and true and find that it is good. For as long as we feel the same after seeing *A Midsummer Night's Dream*, Shakespeare's deeper magic continues to work on us.

NOTES

NOTES

NOTES

A Midsummer Night's Dream

CLIFFSCOMPLETE REVIEW

Use this CliffsComplete Review to gauge what you've learned and to build confidence in your understanding of the original text. After you work through the review questions, the problem-solving exercises, and the suggested activities, you're well on your way to understanding and appreciating the works of William Shakespeare.

Identify The Quotation

Identify the following quotations by answering these questions:

a. Who is the speaker of the quotation?

b. Where does it occur within the play?

c. What does the quotation reveal about the speaker's character?

1. Be advised, fair maid.
   To your father you should be as a god.

2. Well moused, lion!

3. Let me play the lion, too.

4. Either death or you I'll find immediately.

5. But we are spirits of another sort.

6. Thisbe, the flowers of odious savours sweet

7. Come, sit thee down upon this flow'ry bed
   While I thy amiable cheeks do coy

8. More strange than true.

9. I see a voice

10. Ill met by moonlight, proud Titania.

True/False

1. T F Thisbe is killed by a lion.

2. T F The Athenian workmen always speak in prose.

3. T F There is a dog in this play.

4. T F Thisbe is a wandering knight.

5. T F Quince is a tailor.

6. T F Hermia is punished by being locked up in a convent.

7. T F Puck can fly round the world in 20 minutes.

8. T F Pyramus is killed by a lion.

9. T F Tom Snout is a tinker.

10. T F Philostrate is Master of the Revels.

11. T F Helena and Hermia have always been rivals.

12. T F The last speech of the play is made by Puck.

13. T F Theseus is fond of hunting.

14. T F A Bergomask is a kind of dance.

15. T F *A Midsummer Night's Dream* is one of Shakespeare's later plays.

Multiple Choice

1. Pyramus is
   a. a lover
   b. a tyrant
   c. a sailor

2. Hermia's father is
   a. Philostrate
   b. Mustardseed
   c. Egeus

3. How many "mechanicals" are there?
   a. four
   b. five
   c. six

4. Lysander plans to run away with Hermia to his
   a. cousin
   b. mother
   c. aunt

5. Neptune is the god of the
   a. moon
   b. stars
   c. sea

6. Philomel is a name for
   a. a magic juice
   b. the nightingale
   c. a song

7. The "King of Shadows" is
   a. Puck
   b. Oberon
   c. Theseus

8. Thisbe compares Pyramus' nose to a
   a. flower
   b. vegetable
   c. cherry

9. Oberon tells Puck that he will recognize Demetrius by his
   a. height
   b. hair
   c. garments

10. "The tongs and the bones" are
    a. kitchen tools
    b. a disease
    c. musical instruments

11. Theseus orders the four sleeping lovers to be woken by the sound of
    a. soft music
    b. hunting horns
    c. shouting

12. Theseus chooses his wedding entertainment from a list given to him by
    a. Philostrate
    b. Egeus
    c. Lysander

13. Quince's first name is
    a. Francis
    b. Tom
    c. Peter

14. Who dreams about a serpent?
    a. Titania
    b. Hermia
    c. Helena

15. Who leads Demetrius and Lysander on a wild goose chase through the woods?
    a. Mustardseed
    b. Puck
    c. Bottom

Fill in the Blank

1. The first scene of the play is set in
_____.

2. The last scene of the play is set in
_____.

3. Hippolyta is Queen of the _____.

4. Theseus is Duke of _____.

5. Wall is played by _____.

6. The bellows-mender is called _____.

7. The alternative name for Robin
Goodfellow is _____.

8. Egeus is the father of _____.

9. Starveling plays the part of _____.

10. Oberon is angry with Titania because she
will not give him her _____.

Discussion

Use the following questions to generate
discussion.

1. What makes people fall in love in real life?
Does *A Midsummer Night's Dream* add
anything to our understanding of love?

2. Which parts of the play are likely to make
a modern audience laugh most? Which
comic elements of the play might be least
attractive to modern audiences?

3. How does Shakespeare present women in
this play? Are they as strong as the male
characters? Are they dominated by their
menfolk, or by men in general?

4. To what extent are any of the characters in
this play realistic?

5. What do songs, music, and dance contribute to the play?

6. What does the play-within-a-play contribute to *A Midsummer Night's Dream*?

7. In your opinion, why does Shakespeare set
most of the action of the play in a wood,
and not in Athens?

8. In what ways are Helena and Hermia alike
and dissimilar? In what way are Demetrius
and Lysander alike and dissimilar?

9. Which is your favorite character or group
of characters in the play? Why?

10. Which are your favorite lines from the
play? Why?

Identifying Play Elements

Find examples of the following elements in the
text of *A Midsummer Night's Dream:*

* Simile (a comparison using 'like' or 'as')

* Metaphor (more than a comparison—when
something is spoken of as if it were something
else)

* Soliloquy (a speech made not to another character but directly to the audience)

* Hyperbole (a highly exaggerated expression)

* Alliteration (the repetition of consonant sounds
for effect)

* Prose (lines which are not poetry)

* Rhyming Couplet (a pair of lines which end in
the same sound)

* Dramatic Irony (when the audience knows something that the character doesn't)

* Bathos (a sudden change of tone from the sub-
lime to the ridiculous)

* Antithesis (opposite words or ideas placed closely
together)

Activities

The following activities can springboard you into further discussions and projects:

1. If possible, see this play performed. Shakespeare wrote his plays for the stage, and it's far easier to understand his work if you see it performed than if you have to bring it to life in your imagination when reading it. Even a flawed production is worth watching: It might be unsatisfying, but it will encourage you to think about why you were disappointed and how the play should have been produced.

2. Working alone or in a group, design a Web site to help students who are reading *A Midsummer Night's Dream*. Begin by making a list of what the site should contain, and then sketch out a plan of how the site would work, starting with a home page and deciding how the other pages link together. To make it easy to navigate, be sure that each page has a clear link back to the home page, on which you should provide a contents section. You might choose to include a background section that puts the play in context and perhaps a page for each of the main characters or groups of characters. You could include a summary of the play, scene by scene. Whatever you choose to do, keep in mind the purpose of the exercise: to create a resource that will help someone like yourself who wants to organize his or her thoughts on the play and gain new insights into its meaning.

3. Imagine that your school is going to put on a production of *A Midsummer Night's Dream*. Keep in mind that some of the audience won't have studied the play, might be new to Shakespeare, and may find his language a little difficult to understand. Create a theatre program—a small booklet that you would distribute to audience members before the show—that could help them enjoy and understand the performance. Remember that an audience doesn't have time to read a lengthy introduction; you have to decide what important points you want to get across, and present them concisely.

4. Imagine that modern newspaper technology had been available at the time the play is set. Produce the front page—and maybe more—of an edition of a newspaper that might have appeared in ancient Athens on the day after the Duke's wedding. You will need to appoint an editor and allocate articles, columns, and features to members of the group.

5. Select a few characters in the play. Choose *one* short quotation for each (made by or about them) that you think best sums up their characters as revealed in the play. Compare results with your classmates, and take a vote, if you wish, to determine which is the best quote for the job.

6. Shakespeare's theatre had very little in the way of scenery, lighting, or special effects. Discuss the ways in which modern technology could be used to increase the atmosphere of magic in a production of *A Midsummer Night's Dream*. Design a set and plan and write out a lighting and special effects script for the play as it might be performed today.

7. Discuss and design appropriate costumes for the different groups of the play's characters.

8. In a group, act out the play-within-a-play. If time allows, learn the lines and put on a proper performance. You might like to add an extra prologue of your own to explain how "The Most Lamentable Comedy and

Most Cruel Death of Pyramus and Thisbe" came to be performed after the wedding of the Duke of Athens. You could give this part to one of the characters who was present at the event, perhaps. If you feel up to it, you could even try writing the prologue in iambic pentameters!

9. Imagine that you were present at the performance of the play-within-a-play. Write a letter to a friend describing what you saw and why it was so comic.

10. Imagine that you are one of the characters in the play. Write a full description of another character as you see him or her, justifying your judgments and comments by using quotations from the text. Include only information that would be available to the character you have chosen to be.

Answers

Identify the Quotation

1. a. Theseus

b. Act I, Scene 1

c. Theseus is advising Hermia to accept her father's ruling that she should marry Demetrius. These lines show his authority and his adherence to the conventions of the time. The suggestion that Hermia should regard Egeus "as a god" is a strong expression of the absoluteness of a father's authority, which makes her rebellion against it seem all the more dramatic.

2. a. Theseus

b. Act V, Scene 1

c. Theseus is commenting on Snug's performance in the play-within-a-play. His remark is a joke, suggesting that Snug's feeble attempts look more like a mouse than a lion. It shows that Theseus has a sense of humor and contributes to the relaxed realism of the last scene of the play.

3. a. Bottom

b. Act I, Scene 2

c. This shows Bottom's childish enthusiasm and vanity: He wants to play all the parts in the play-within-a-play.

4. a. Hermia

b. Act II, Scene 2

c. When Hermia wakes to discover that Lysander has disappeared, she expresses her anxiety in a characteristically extreme way, emphasizing the absolute and obsessive nature of young love. Her expression underlines the all-or-nothing view of life and love, and the word "immediately" suggests her impatience.

5. a. Oberon

b. Act III, Scene 2

c. Oberon is speaking to Puck, but his remark reminds the audience that fairies are not the same kind of spirits as ghosts and "damned spirits," which are creatures of darkness.

6. a. Bottom (as Pyramus)

b. Act III, Scene 1

c. Bottom makes one of his mistakes with language here. The word he should use is "odorous," meaning (sweet) smelling; he uses "odious," meaning hateful. This is one of many examples of his stupidity.

7. a. Titania

b. Act IV, Scene 1

c. These words express the delicate sweetness of Titania's magic-induced love for Bottom and show an affectionate side to her character. The lines are absurdly comic when addressed by the Queen of the Fairies to a crude human with an ass's head.

8. a. Theseus

b. Act V, Scene 1

c. Theseus and Hippolyta are discussing the story told to them by the four young lovers. The strong, practical, and decisive Theseus is disinclined to believe what he has been told, whereas Hippolyta thinks it strangely credible. Their opinions on this matter could be taken as alternative views of the impact of *A Midsummer Night's Dream* on the audience.

9. a. Bottom (as Pyramus)

b. Act V, Scene 1

c. Another example of Bottom's verbal clumsiness. He repeatedly gets his senses mixed up—a running joke in the play.

10. a. Oberon

b. Act II, Scene 1

c. This is the first line spoken by Oberon, and it makes clear from the start that he and his wife are at odds. He calls her "proud," suggesting that they have argued over something and she has refused to give in to him. The line contains one of the play's many references to moonlight, instantly associating the fairy world with its silvery light.

True/False

1. False 2. False 3. True 4. False 5. False 6. False 7. False 8. False 9. True 10. True 11. False 12. True 13. True 14. True 15. False

Multiple Choice

1. a 2. c 3. c 4. c 5. c 6. b 7. b 8. c 9. c 10. c 11. b 12. a 13. c 14. b 15. b

Fill in the Blank

1. Athens 2. Athens 3. Amazons 4. Athens 5. Snout 6. Flute 7. Puck 8. Hermia 9. Moonshine 10. Indian boy

CLIFFSCOMPLETE RESOURCE CENTER

The learning doesn't need to stop here. Cliffs-Complete Resource Center shows you the best of the best: great links to information in print, on film, and online. And the following aren't all the great resources available to you; visit www.cliffsnotes.com for tips on reading literature, writing papers, giving presentations, locating other resources, and testing your knowledge.

BOOKS

Bullough, Geoffrey. *Narrative and Dramatic Sources of Shakespeare.* New York: Columbia University Press, 1972.

This a good resource for those students keen to explore Shakespeare's sources.

Dover Wilson, John. *Life in Shakespeare's England.* Cambridge University Press, 1911.

This text, reissued by Penguin Books Inc. in 1944, is currently out of print. Good libraries will have this, and you may be able to buy it second-hand. It is a marvelous anthology of writings by Shakespeare's contemporaries, which gives a detailed picture of what it must have been like to live in Early Modern England, and which helps the modern student understand the context in which the plays were written and performed.

Doyle, John and Ray Lischner. *Shakespeare For Dummies.* Foster City, California: Hungry Minds, Inc., 1999.

This guide to Shakespeare's plays and poetry provides summaries and scorecards for keeping track of who's who in a given play, as well as painless introductions to language, imagery, and other often intimidating subjects.

Dutton, Richard (ed.). *Shakespeare, A Midsummer Night's Dream: A Casebook.* London: Palgrave, 1996.

This collection of critical essays and extracts will be useful to the more advanced student.

INTERNET

"Illinois Shakespeare Festival."

www.orat.ilstu.edu/shakespeare

This site features an attractively presented range of resources including essays and play reviews. There is a good article by Scott Walters about the different ways in which the fairies *in A Midsummer Night's Dream* have been represented in various productions throughout the years.

"Mr. William Shakespeare and the Internet"

daphne.palomar.edu/shakespeare

This site aims to be a complete annotated guide to the scholarly Shakespeare resources available on the Internet. It has many excellent links and also includes resources of more general use, such as details of Shakespeare festivals.

"Webspeare"

cncn.com/homepages/ken_m/shakespeare.html

This site is aimed at high school students and their teachers. Among its many useful and attractive features is a section devoted to teaching the proper pronunciation of Elizabethan English, with easily downloadable sound files as examples.

"A Midsummer Night's Dream"

www.foxsearchlight.com/midfinal

This resource, based upon the Michael Hoffman film, has downloadable study notes and exercises in Adobe Acrobat format.

FILMS

There are several readily available movies of *A Midsummer Night's Dream*, and though each of them will be of interest to students, they all have weaknesses as well as strengths.

Hoffman, Michael. *A Midsummer Night's Dream.* 20th Century Fox, 1999.

This version is an "all star" movie with the action transferred to nineteenth-century Tuscany. It is visually beautiful and makes the story accessible, but not everybody thinks it does justice to the play.

Noble, Adrian. *A Midsummer Night's Dream.* Miramax, 1996.

This film version of a Royal Shakespeare Company production is intelligent and impressive, but it does contain some theatrical devices that might confuse students new to the play. For example, the wood near Athens is represented as a bare wooden floor, and some of the actors play more than one character.

Reinhardt, Max. *A Midsummer Night's Dream.* Warner, 1935.

This movie, starring James Cagney as Bottom and Mickey Rooney as Puck, is a dated but Oscar-winning adaptation and is good in parts. It includes the classic Mendelssohn music.

You might also be able to get a copy of the video of the 1988 BBC production of the play, directed by Elijah Moshinsky and produced by Jonathan Miller. The BBC also produced a short cartoon version of *A Midsummer Night's Dream*, directed by Robert Saakiants, in its *Shakespeare— The Animated Tales* series. The text is heavily abridged, but the story comes across clearly.

OTHER MEDIA

A Midsummer Night's Dream. Audio CD (unabridged). Naxos Audio Books, 1997.

This well reviewed audio CD features Warren Mitchell, Michael Maloney, and Sarah Woodward.

SHAKSPER Listserv **SHAKSPER@ws.bowiestate.edu**

This is an international electronic conference for Shakespearean researchers, instructors, students, and those who share their academic interests and concerns. For further details, e-mail the moderator, Dr. Hardy M. Cook, at the above address.

CLIFFSCOMPLETE READING GROUP DISCUSSION GUIDE

Use the following questions and topics to enhance your reading group discussions. The discussion can help get you thinking—and hopefully talking—about Shakespeare in a whole new way!

Discussion Questions

1. In many productions of *A Midsummer Night's Dream,* the text is heavily cut, some key characters are omitted, and a great deal of extra music, dancing, and special effects are added. Why do you think a producer would make these changes? What elements (if any) of Shakespeare's original play could be enhanced by such changes? What would be lost if, for example, the mechanicals and the play-within-a-play were cut out?

2. Many films and stage productions have set Shakespeare's plays in time periods and locations different from those specified by Shakespeare himself. For example, productions of *Julius Caesar* have been set in Nazi Germany, a 1930s Chicago meat-packing factory, and even in outer space. The most recent movie version of *A Midsummer Night's Dream* is set not in ancient Athens, as Shakespeare intended, but in late nineteenth-century Italy. What (if anything) can be gained by such changes, and what (if anything) lost?

3. Bottom is proud, vain, self-important, and ignorant. Nonetheless, throughout the ages, the best actors have longed to play him, and audiences and readers are fascinated by him. Why is this? To what extent does Shakespeare invite us to laugh with him as well as at him?

4. "Lord, what fools these mortals be!" To what extent is Puck's judgment justified by the events of the play?

5. The story of Pyramus and Thisbe is essentially a tragic one, and it is told as a tragedy in the sources through which Shakespeare knew it. In *A Midsummer Night's Dream,* however, the events of the tale are presented in a way that makes us laugh at them. How seriously are the other loves treated in Shakespeare's play? Is Shakespeare celebrating love, mocking it, or both?

6. What is love? Do we understand the idea of love any better after seeing *A Midsummer Night's Dream?*

7. Attending plays was not just the privilege of the upper classes in Shakespeare's time. His audiences were mixed and included not only the educated but also the "groundlings"—poorer folk who paid a small sum to watch the play while standing. Which elements of this play would have appealed to the groundlings? Which elements may have gone over their heads? Which parts of the play would go over the heads of most members of a modern audience who might not have studied the play before watching it? How much does this matter?

8. The philosopher Wittgenstein said, "A dream is all wrong . . . and yet at the same time it is completely right." How well does *A Midsummer Night's Dream* manage to be both dream-like and realistic at the same time?

9. The critic William Hazlitt wrote, "Fairies are not incredible, but fairies six feet high are so." Does the fact that few people believe in fairies these days get in the way of our appreciation of *A Midsummer Night's Dream?* Modern productions of the play have had fairies dressed as Hell's Angels, half-naked, all in white, or all in black. Is it better to present the fairies in the conventional "ballerina" style or to have them dressed more strangely or even sinisterly?

10. How would you defend the play against the judgment of the diarist Samuel Pepys, who said in 1662 that *A Midsummer Night's Dream* was "the most insipid, ridiculous play that ever I saw in my life"?

NOTES

NOTES

Index

continued

continued

M

Q

R